HOPE
for Survivors of
Childhood Trauma

A PERSONAL STORY AND A
LIFE-CHANGING PROGRAM

Susan M. Conord

HOPE for Survivors of Childhood Trauma
by Susan M. Conord

Printed in the United States of America

ISBN 978-1-60791-383-2

www.xulonpress.com

Then Samuel took a stone and set it up between Mizpah and Shen. He named it Ebenezer, saying, "Thus far has the Lord helped us."

I Samuel 7:12

Author's Foreword and Acknowledgements

Everyone has a story and the following is my story. Without the experiences I had growing up and then crashing and burning at the age of thirty-five, there would not be an Ebenezer program. I would have had no understanding of what it is to grow up in a place that did not feel safe and with caregivers who had so many challenges of their own that parenting me was more than they could manage.

I've heard it said that God never uses anyone in a mighty way until first He breaks them all to pieces. There may be some truth in that. When my buried childhood caught up with me in mid-life, I experienced the awakening like a fall from the cliffs. I know, though, that before I was to hit the bottom, He clothed me in some kind of parachute and saved my life.

This breakdown of mine was perhaps the first thing in my life I couldn't control or at least think I was in some way "fixing". I had lived my life up until then white-knuckling and clenching the threads to keep the fabric from tearing. Everything was lined up every moment to reassure myself that I was safe, the world was safe. Without even knowing what I was doing, I was leaning on a thick metal door to prevent myself from feeling and seeing what was buried so deep inside. By my mid-thirties, the metal had started to rust and when we made a move to New Jersey in 1986, the upheaval to me and my family ripped it all wide open. The journey back from that plunge is what this story is about.

I did not start writing the Ebenezer material until thirteen years later and really only intended to create a Bible Study that would focus on the devastation and recovery from a difficult childhood. It never entered my mind that this would become a program that would reach across towns and change so many lives, including my own. The word "awesome" is overused these days, but in the true sense of the word, the experience of writing this material was one that had me vibrating with awe. The words flowed from me like waves tumbling and splashing to make their way to the page. I never in my life have felt so much like a vessel, His waters sliding through me like a living liquid. As much as I would love to take credit for this program, I never felt that it belonged to me. My God has moved and shaped me right along with the many that have gone through the Ebenezer program. I, too, am different as a result of His Truth.

There are many to thank for bringing this program and this book to light. I'm indebted to the authors whose works influenced me and supported my own recovery from the past. Sandra D. Wilson wrote one of the finest books on shame that I have ever read. Dr. Henry Cloud and Dr. John Townsend gave me much to chew on in the area of personal boundaries, and Gray Smalley's work on emotional intimacy and marriage issues changed my own marriage. The insights from all of these authors found their way into Ebenezer.

Beyond that are the many who have traveled through the program, their hearts bumping up against mine and changing and challenging me in multiple ways. Together we learned how to drop the mask of perfectionism, isolation and image management. We became less afraid and more willing to know and be known. We found out that we were not alone in our suffering; that there are others whose stories, while different in detail, are just as devastating and carry far reaching effects so much like our own. To know that there are others like us is one of the first revelations that free us from the prison in which we grew up, where secrets and the "No Talk" rule kept us silent and alone. The kindness and empathy that is born each year in these groups is something to behold. Strangers in the first class become sisters by class twenty.

There were many who encouraged, maybe even hounded me, to get this book together and finished, and I am so thankful they believed it could be done. I have to thank dear Cynthia White who spent long hours inputting the material into a usable format. My friend, Christiane Carlson-Thies, was always ready to discuss ideas and read through what I had written and could be counted on to tell me the truth. I have to thank my daughter, Kate Leavell, who provided photographs, and her friend Stacy, whose daughter posed for the cover photo. And, of course, my wonderful husband, Michael Conord, who stood by me all these years as my story unfolded and then did some very helpful editing and goading me on to finish.

And where would this program and this book be if my God were not God? My pains, struggles, recovery and the privilege of passing this on would simply not be. Without His grace to save and His mercy to heal, the story would have begun and ended in hell. Instead, the story is brimming with what we need most in this world: *hope.*

TABLE OF CONTENTS

FOREWARD

Susan Conord has walked through the valley. The worst part of her journey was feeling the aloneness. The best part was God's blessing her as she opened herself up to Him, *I am yours, make me whole*. But there's more to the story. She started to put together a Bible study to give hope to other childhood abuse survivors. The study turned into a program, which brings together Scripture, common sense and counseling concepts from Christian and secular sources. She also listened to the women who went through her study and used their feedback to revise this work. I have personally talked with some of her graduates and seen the fruit of changed lives.

Susan's approach is academically and scripturally sound, but her credentials are experiential and not academic, which makes her story easily read and the Ebenezer program's approach and concepts easily grasped. The focus is for the participants in the program to do the work of healing and drop the masks that keep us isolated. If you have grown up with alcoholism, abuse, severe neglect or other family dysfunction, then reading Susan's story and working through Ebenezer is an excellent way to recover and experience God's healing mercies.

Mark C. Good, Ph.D.
Board Certified Diplomate in Clinical Social Work

My Story of Recovery

Chapter 1

I remember the day my life turned upside down with unusual clarity; the emotions, the smells, the physical feelings; waves of irritation and anger swirling into tormenting fear; sodden, earthy, humidity, the pungency of tennis ball rubber, and dizzy surges of nausea. One moment I was the "old" me and the next, a whole series of dramatic changes were set in motion that would alter the world as I had known it-would, in fact, alter the core of my own being.

But what happened to me didn't really begin that day in July 1987. That day in July was only the explosion, the outward manifestation at long last of an entire mountain of pain carried within me since childhood. It seems odd that I could live with such a sizable wound and be totally unaware of its existence. But I have since come to appreciate the mysteries of the complex people God has created and the amazing coping strategies we adopt in order to survive trauma.

I grew up, for the most part, an only child because my sister, born thirteen months after me, came prematurely and suffered profound brain damage and blindness. She was institutionalized by age two, the same time my mother was hospitalized for a breakdown and alcoholism. My sister, Ann, remained in institutions and my father moved near the psychiatric hospital to be near my mother. I lived with my grandparents for five years until my mother and father and I began again as a family when I was eight years old. I had always remembered us as being a "normal" family, very close, happy. We were the "second-chance" family—the family that had bounced back and made it work. I had no idea before that series of awakening jolts in July how very far off the mark my memories were.

When I was sixteen, eight years after my mother, father and I were re-united, my father died suddenly in a boating accident. He left home that day to change the oil on the motor of his twenty-two foot sailboat, built by his own hands over a ten year period. When he didn't return that evening, my mother and I hoped he had found his way to a bar with some drinking buddies. The next morning, though, the call came. His beloved boat had washed ashore on Kent Island. Three days later his body was found.

I had remembered him as being the funny guy, laughing, good-time Daddy.

The fact that we had never had one serious conversation in those sixteen years, that he had been totally uninvolved in my life, that he had never attended my cheerleading events, come to see me in the hospital when I'd had my tonsils removed or given me fatherly discipline or guidance had simply been deleted from my mind. Anyway, my experience was "normal"; it was all I knew. It was later in life when I discovered what I had missed: the bottle was his child, his wife, his master, but my subconscious chose not to see.

When I was twenty-three my mother, too, died suddenly. She had been diagnosed as suffering from viral pneumonia one week before being rushed to the hospital where she died before I was even told that she had been admitted. A blood-clot had claimed her at the age of forty-nine. My Mama was gone and something inside me died with her. We had been so close and I had lived to shine for her. In fact, I was very enmeshed with her. Never experiencing normal teen-age rebellion and always looking to please, I didn't understand the personhood I had surrendered in order to be loved. The trauma and abandonment, the multitude of losses as a young child, left me afraid; terrified of so many things.

From all outward appearances I took these deaths in stride, failing however, to deal with the deadness within me. I was a Christian by this time and I believed the scriptures that told me that my God would never leave me alone, my greatest fear. Just after my father's death, when I was sixteen, I was presented with a redeeming and loving Jesus at a huge conference in Atlantic City, New Jersey.

My concept of God until then had been a distant, uninvolved being. I pictured Him a powerful force, impersonal and maybe loving, maybe not. This Jesus I encountered at the conference was different from everything I had imagined. He wasn't just powerful; He was real, He was personal and He was loving. Everyone powerful in my life until then had been distracted, depressed and out of control. I was abandoned over and over again when my alcoholic parents could barely navigate their own lives. I was surrendered to grandparents when I was three-a time so black and terrifying I blocked out long segments of time. Then, the ultimate abandonment when my parents took me home when I was eight years old and the world really went crazy. So to discover a God who promised to love me and never leave was a revelation that captured me. When my father died so suddenly, it was, of course, another abandonment for me. Someone, this Jesus, was finally saying I was lovable and worth sticking around for. For me, at sixteen, that Jesus merited taking the risk of belief. That step of belief began a life-time of following and getting to know God.

At that time, though, I knew nothing about grieving and very little about this God I had decided to follow. I thought grieving was showing lack of acceptance for God's plan so, at sixteen, when my father died and later, when I was twenty-three and my mother suddenly died, I buried my feelings along with my parents. This, too, would catch up with me that sultry day in July.

Chapter 2

That devastating summer came after we moved from Maryland to New Jersey. "We" now included my husband, Michael, and our three children. Making that move was one of the hardest decisions we had ever made as a couple. As Assistant Pastor in our Annapolis church, Michael had started an evening service in a barn (complete with the usual barny aromas), that had grown and prospered to be a church of 600 people with a staff of three pastors. We had nurtured and loved those people for ten years and they were my family. Except for college and seminary, we had grown up and lived in the Annapolis-Severna Park area for twenty years. This was home!

When the pulpit committee from New Jersey called, I was caught off-guard. Though we had many times talked of moving to another small ministry to begin again and watch the Lord create a church, somehow the inertia of being "home" and the difficulties of making a move and uprooting our family had kept us from acting out our daydreams.

Even as we received that phone call, I was in the middle of teaching a women's Bible study to over 100 women on the subject of self-esteem and identity in Christ. Through my study and teaching I had experienced a burst of emotional and spiritual growth. I was learning a trust in people, and openness to intimacy in relationships that was new to me. As I read and studied, I found myself immersed in the wonder of God's love for me and His acceptance of me as a unique person. The message He gave me was simply that my self-esteem and identity came from Him and His view of me—not the media, the world's values, old voices in my head or other people. As my inner self began to open up and be known, the "Pastor's Wife" pedestal that I had teetered upon, made of other people's expectations, began to dissolve. Moving now seemed very untimely. But I had known the Lord long enough to trust His leading and it seemed more and more obvious to my husband and me that God was calling us to that little church in New Jersey. I had no idea that one of the reasons He was calling us there was to give me a place to be broken all to pieces.

So we moved that March, only four months after receiving the first phone call from the pulpit committee. And the bottom dropped out of my world. Looking back, it's clear that I was crumbling inside, but at the time, I thought I was not only holding myself together but everything and everyone else as well.

Nothing, but nothing, was coming easily. In fact, nothing was working out at all! When my old friends from Maryland contacted me, they assumed all would be sweet. We had followed the Lord's call and He would reward us by making clear paths for our feet. I told them we were, instead, over-run with troubles. How naïve and narrow our thinking can be! The house we bought was a handy-man special, a huge Victorian disaster that begged to be restored. No problem! Always a woman of vision, I had no trouble seeing the tidy English garden that would bloom in the back, the charming butler's pantry where I would serve elegant meals, the glowing floors and sparkling brass that would soon emerge. What I *didn't* see were the carpenter ants, the water, the rot, the roof, the leaning garage, the flying squirrels crawling in the walls and chewing the wiring. And that's only a partial listing of the nightmares we faced and the expenses incurred. And I did not know that my husband would be thrown into a difficult and wretched situation as he took the call to this new church. He would have his own experience of being broken.

At the same time, the children were suffering. We were in a "bedroom community" twenty miles outside New York City and the atmosphere of our town was as electric, competitive, tense, and driven as the city itself. The lines from the old song, referring to New York, "If you can make it there, you can make it anywhere" took on new meaning for me. Every day the children would come home from school weeping and begging to go "home." Our youngest daughter, Kate, a fourth grader, pretended to be coping but she closed up inside herself. Our son, David, in the 6th grade, told us repeatedly how much he hated New Jersey and wrote long letters to his old friends. Sarah, our eldest, was in the eighth grade and became the class scapegoat. She was verbally and emotionally abused by her aggressive classmates and ended each day in tears. David started having anxiety attacks at bedtime that would throw him into such a panic that we could hardly quiet him. And I continued to believe that everything *had* to be all right or I must *make* it all right. I would be strong no matter what transpired and it never, ever occurred to me to ask for help.

The church we came to serve posed another challenge for me. This church was in pain. The situation preceding our call had wounded many in the congregation and they were still reeling from their hurts. The two previous pastors had suffered nervous breakdowns and a divorce. Though the church made every effort to welcome us warmly, still I sensed an undercurrent of reserve and fear. It would take time for these dear people to come to know us and to trust us. It became apparent, too, that many in this tiny group were suffering long term personal pains. Being a mother-hen who came thinking I was going to enfold these hurting people to my bosom and love the hurt away, I took the church on in what I later came to see as a messiah role. But this anguish and these woes were deeper than I knew, and my frustration and feeling of failure mounted. I was completely unaware of my own gaping wounds and unaddressed issues.

All the while that I was being overwhelmed with disorder, I was working very hard to make these fragmented pieces come together into some kind of wholeness. Feeling totally responsible to make a home out of the rubble, soothe the children, and prop up my hurting husband, I physically worked myself to exhaustion: wallpapering, digging, dragging, until late at night. In the back of my mind I was vaguely aware that I was feeling a certain driven-ness to get things settled, to get them right. But I chose not to explore what was happening to me because that would mean stopping, and there seemed no way I could do that.

Feeling the expectations of the congregation, I took on leading and teaching roles in the church while trying to comfort the children and instill positive attitudes toward our new life. All of this, of course, sandwiched in between the continuing struggle to tame the house into a home. Sometimes I would sob in the basement while I folded clothes between bouts of hanging wallpaper, but mostly I just kept going. It never occurred to me that there were any other options! I believed that if it must be done, it can be done.

During this time I started to wake during the night feeling incredibly anxious, my heart beating wildly, and a feeling like electric current crawling up the back of my neck and head. This had happened once in Maryland during the period when we struggled to make our decision about the move and at the time I had dismissed the event as a drug reaction to antihistamines.

These odd episodes began to happen more frequently-several a week- and then I began to experience them during the day. Out of nowhere, the physical symptoms coupled with overwhelming fear, would slither over me. Something felt terribly wrong but I had no idea what it was, only that I felt helpless and in danger. At the same time, the driven-ness I had been feeling became harder to control. I felt as though I would burst if I couldn't get things in order, things to work right, things finished. Finally something happened that made me realize this was big. My husband and I were working in the front yard and Michael sprayed the hose on the new outdoor lamp and I screamed at him in annoyance. NOW I would have to get paper towels out and dry off the water spots! When he pointed out that it got rained on all the time, I felt as though I had been shaken awake. I was caught in the unreasonable expectation that everything had to be perfectly in control, flawless, and I was responsible to make it happen. I couldn't stop. I had to "get it right." But "it" had become a jumbled acreage of imperfections that never let me rest. Still I had no idea what was wrong or what to do about what was happening to me.

How strange it seems to me now to have been so independent and isolated that these frightening things were happening in my life and I carried them alone. I never asked for help; I never said "I can't." I didn't even admit fully to Michael the magnitude of my fear and these strange episodes of panic because I didn't fully admit them to myself. But I knew I was in trouble and I began asking God to rescue me. I asked Him to take this driven-ness demon away from me and I think what I wanted was a wave of a magic wand and to be instantly and painlessly released from bondage. I had no idea that pain was what drove me, and no idea at all of the work God was about to begin in my life.

If I HAD known ahead, I would have run as far as I could from His hand! But He gave me no choice and in His wisdom He began a soul surgery that would last two years and would save my life. As I look back now, I continually thank God for the miracle of being freed from a prison that was invisible to me; a prison I had grown so accustomed to that I never knew the fresh air I had been missing. If I had to choose whether I would remain my "old" self before my breakdown or go through the torture I experienced, there would really be no choice to make. After knowing this freedom, this health, I would never, never go back. Yes, I'd go through it again. But if I had been asked to take this journey that July, my answer would have been quite different. God, in His wisdom, chose for me.

Chapter 3

It was incredibly hot—high 90's with matching humidity. Michael had promised me a tennis game at six, but when he came home, he wisely suggested we forego the match. I was worried about my elevated blood pressure, though, and insisted I needed the exercise. And I was angry that he didn't want to play, but being one who rarely expressed my anger, I kept the intensity to myself. We played in the muggy heat on empty stomachs, and walking back to the car, I felt seasick. Some of the odd anxiety feeling mixed with nausea and dizziness overcame me when we reached home and I couldn't face eating the dinner I had struggled to prepare.

The next day I threw up and was so nauseated I decided it must be a stomach virus. But I felt peculiar—something wasn't right. I sipped Ginger Ale, but couldn't even choke down dry toast. By the third day I was no better and I became so weak that I was slipping away. My doctor was alarmed when we called and ordered us immediately to her office. I remember, somewhat fuzzily, Michael carrying me into the waiting room. As if in a fog, I was disconnected from my body—we were no longer the cozy duo we had always been.

The doctor sent me to the hospital where blood tests revealed I had developed diabetes. I was released the next day with a diet prescription and so much confusion to add to my fear and other burdens. How could I have diabetes? Always a healthy person, suddenly I had a life-threatening disease along with episodes of racing heart and tingling limbs.

It was several weeks later that I began to be very thirsty and to urinate what seemed to be copious quarts. I began to feel light-headed and the doctor once more ordered me to the hospital. Tests showed no sugar in my urine, though a thorough glucose screening two weeks after my diabetes was first discovered confirmed that I did indeed have the disease. With no explanation for what was happening to me, I was admitted for further tests. Fear mounted as I was taken to the floor treating critical heart problems, wired to an alarm system should my heart beat erratically and an attack be imminent. I had a strange choking sensation in my breast-bone/esophagus area. Suddenly breathing became difficult—what had been a natural function, never before studied, now became a struggle. I was given oxygen for frequent light-headedness and stabbed with countless needles. Tests were run for various rare kidney diseases, tumors, pancreatic disorders, stomach disorders, blood disorders, and heart problems of every sort. Every test came up negative and I felt relief mixed with growing fear. What WAS wrong with me? At about the same time, I stopped being able to digest food. Whatever went in came out in the same form. Now I was truly frightened.

All my life I had been good old dependable me. Strong as an ox, tough as nails. Now I was exhausted. I'd never in my life felt so tired. This was bottom-of-the-well tiredness that seemed never to abate no matter how much I rested. It was the kind of tired that hurt. I dropped close to fifteen pounds, was constantly nauseated, had pain in my chest and difficulty breathing as though I had swallowed a huge rock and it was lodged there. I was fainting, had been diagnosed a diabetic, could no longer digest the little food I was able to get down, and I was feeling haunted and hunted by anxiety. I had become a stranger to myself.

After being in the hospital for a week of endless testing, my doctor came to sit with me. I'll never forget her tender look of concern as she concluded that there was nothing organically wrong with me. She said gently that I was suffering from "stress."

Stress! Was she crazy? I was sick! I had diabetes, malabsorption, trouble breathing, pain, nausea—how could that be caused by stress? How ignorant I was! What I didn't know is how mysteriously and inextricably linked are the physical human body and its emotions. My body was breaking down from too much overload for too long.

I remember feeling intensely embarrassed that the diagnosis wasn't organic and that I was labeled "mentally sick." This to me was weakness and weakness wasn't allowed. Even then, with a gentle and concerned doctor at my side, I was unable to ask for help and to fully allow myself to see the fear I had dammed up within myself. I wanted to be released to go home immediately.

Released to WHAT I didn't know, but I was desperate to get out. My doctor recommended a psychologist to me; she said I needed to be talking to someone. But about what, I wondered? Everything had been tough but it was getting better and I was all right. It seemed that the worst of my troubles had been the physical problems that had brought my life to a sudden halt.

When I arrived home, I went to the bedroom to lie down and there I experienced the most dreadful, fully felt panic attack I had ever known. Flung into the utter horror of total unleashed terror, there was no bottom, no reality, and I feared I was losing my mind. I felt as if I had disintegrated into a million pieces. No molecules held together anymore. Life wasn't life anymore. I wasn't me anymore. The attack passed but the experience left me fearing for my life.

Chapter 4

I wish I had kept a journal during those hot August days. They blur together in my memory; just a hazy existence, a waking nightmare. Both Michael and I stubbornly clung to the belief that my troubles were physical and my doctor continued to gently insist they were emotionally caused.

I was so weak and thin and constantly plagued with waves of nausea. Sometimes the nausea would pass for an hour or so and I'd be desperate to eat something, to get some calories into this body wasting away before my eyes. All my life I had fought chubbiness and so it was strange to be now frightened of literally starving to death. And I was so incredibly tired. There were no reserves left. Even when I woke in the morning, the dragging, painful depths of exhaustion held me.

Until my hospitalization, my blood pressure had been erratic and high, but it mysteriously plummeted to normal after I arrived home and experienced that panic attack. It was as though my body and soul had screamed out a blood-curdling cry of "I can't" for the first time in my life, and the ceaseless striving came to a forced stop. Always I had been able to be and to do what I needed to be and do. My motto was, "If it MUST be done, it CAN be done" and in my heart of hearts, I believed this to be true. There would be some terrible consequence if I failed—fuzzy and undetermined, but terrible and swift.

It was so bizarre to say, "I can't."—the feelings were jumbled and contradictory. I was scared—this "I can't" stuff made me so dependent on others. Would they help me? Would they resent me? Would they lose respect for me? Would they be angry at me for letting them down? Would I be alone? And what about all the things I valued and had labored for? What would happen to my home, my garden, my ministries?

But somewhere deep within there was also a sense of relief, as I awakened to the knowledge that this incredible load I had always carried had become burdensome. I realized that this boulder ("made up of what?" I asked, but as yet I had no answers), this boulder I had pushed up an endless incline, had finally slipped from my grasp. Though it had rolled over me and nearly pressed the life from me, still it was rolling *away* and I no longer shouldered that cruel load.

Chapter 5

I am amazed that I managed to function at all in those days. Life was reduced to the essentials and I found myself rethinking my basic values as they were held up to close scrutiny. Though before reading the Bible and prayer had long been a daily and continuous channel of communication between God and me, the Bible and prayer now became as essential as breathing. Before, I spent that time more out of duty because I thought it was what I was *supposed* to do. Now, I sat for hours with the Bible open on my lap, searching His words, crying and begging Him for mercy. God gave me a special measure of faith and I never doubted His presence— but I was afraid of what he was taking me through.

At first, escape from pain was my only goal. I had no understanding of WHAT was happening to me let along WHY it was happening!

One day, as I read the third chapter of Lamentations, it was as though my heart was laid bare on that page:

> I am the man who has seen affliction
> by the rod of his wrath.
> He has driven me away and made me walk
> in darkness rather than light;
> indeed, he has turned his hand against me.
> again and again, all day long.
> He has made my skin and my flesh grow old
> and has broken my bones.
> He has besieged me and surrounded me
> with bitterness and hardship.

He has made me dwell in darkness

like those long dead.

He has walled me in so I cannot escape;

he has weighed me down with chains.

Even when I call out or cry for help,

he shuts out my prayer.

He has barred my way with blocks of stone;

he has made my paths crooked.

Like a bear lying in wait,

like a lion in hiding,

he dragged me from the path and mangled me

and left me without help.

He drew his bow

and made me the target for his arrows.

He pierced my heart

with arrows from his quiver.

I became the laughingstock of all my people;

they mock me in song all day long.

He has filled me with bitter herbs

and sated me with gall.

He has broken my teeth with gravel;

he has trampled me in the dust.

I have been deprived of peace;

I have forgotten what prosperity is.

So I say, "My splendor is gone

and all that I had hoped from the LORD."

I remember my affliction and my wandering,

the bitterness and the gall.

I well remember them,

and my soul is downcast within me.

How perfectly these verses expressed my pain and confusion. My strength was gone and resting brought no relief so there was nothing I could do anymore. My beauty was gone; I was sickly thin, and I could pull the waistband of my skirt all the way over my now non-existent breasts up to my chin. My face was haggard with dark circles under my eyes. I felt walled in with no escape. I felt humiliated to be so weak and afraid. Being a pastor's wife meant having a very PUBLIC breakdown. There would be no slinking off in a corner for me. I was forced from the beginning to expose myself and the shame I felt to anyone who would look. Later I would see that this too was God's loving design for my healing. Without this forced exposure I would have chosen to hide and thereby forfeited what God had to give me.

Lamentations goes on and day by day my healing went on as well.

> Yet this I call to mind
> and therefore I have hope:
> Because of the LORD's great love we are not consumed,
> for his compassions never fail.
> They are new every morning;
> great is your faithfulness.
> I say to myself, "The LORD is my portion;
> therefore I will wait for him."
> The LORD is good to those whose hope is in him,
> to the one who seeks him;
> it is good to wait quietly
> for the salvation of the LORD.

Much later verse 56 would be my cry:

> You heard my plea: "Do not close your ears
> to my cry for relief."
> You came near when I called you,
> and you said, "Do not fear."

God began to teach me to WAIT—there was no escape from my illness or my pain and no way to "fix" what was happening to me because I didn't understand what was happening. There was no running for me—I was too sick so there was only clinging to the Lord and waiting for Him. He began to teach me that even if we go to the very depths of pain and "hell", He is there.

After Lamentations, I began to re-study Job. I had only recently taught this book, but I had taught it so naively. Now the pages came alive for me and I was overcome with empathy for Job and a new understanding of myself and my God.

It was the last five chapters that God used to sear my heart. I had begged the Lord to stop the pain and physical disintegration because what I wanted most was to be comfortable and well. His response to me came in these chapters of Job:

> "Who is this that darkens my counsel
>
> with words without knowledge?
>
> Brace yourself like a man;
>
> I will question you,
>
> and you shall answer me.
>
> "Where were you when I laid the earth's foundation?
>
> Tell me, if you understand…
>
> Have the gates of death been shown to you?
>
> Have you seen the gates of the shadow of death?
>
> Have you comprehended the vast expanses of the earth?
>
> Tell me, if you know all this.
>
> "What is the way to the abode of light?
>
> And where does darkness reside?
>
> Can you take them to their places?
>
> Do you know the paths to their dwellings?
>
> Surely you know, for you were already born!
>
> You have lived so many years!…
>
> "Will the one who contends with the Almighty correct him?
>
> Let him who accuses God answer him!"

And with those words, my pride and my real inability to wait for God in trusting submission, wholly given to His plan over my own, was laid bare for me to see. My God was at work on REAL health—my inner self was undergoing surgery by the Great Physician and I was running from the operating table at full tilt! I was the woman riddled with worms who wanted a warm, cozy afghan to make me feel better.

If God was my God, then I owed Him my submission. If He was the loving father I believed Him to be, then I owed Him my trust. Even in pain and no matter what He desired to take me through. Would I let God be God? Could I say, "Even though he slay me, yet will I trust Him"? Job 13:15

Job's moment of clarity in the last chapter expressed the clearer vision God granted me:

> "I know that you can do all things;
>
> no plan of yours can be thwarted.
>
> You asked, 'Who is this that obscures my counsel without knowledge?'
>
> Surely I spoke of things I did not understand,
>
> things too wonderful for me to know.
>
> "You said, 'Listen now, and I will speak;
>
> I will question you,
>
> and you shall answer me.'
>
> My ears had heard of you
>
> but now my eyes have seen you.
>
> Therefore I despise myself
>
> and repent in dust and ashes."

From that moment on, my prayers changed from "Take this away" to **"I am yours, make me whole."**

Chapter 6

I began to care for myself. I had to get well, so I ate the carefully prescribed diabetic diet, fighting the nausea. I slept as much as I could, a nap every afternoon and regular bedtimes. Falling asleep was not a problem, but staying blissfully unconscious was impossible. I would awaken suddenly during the early morning hours, feeling that odd and uncomfortable anxiousness.

And I began to walk. At first I was so weak that just to go as far as a couple of blocks took everything I had. Slowly, though, this improved and I worked out a regular pattern of walking every morning and then again in the afternoon or evening.

It felt strange to make such an important task out of caring for myself. It was such a contrast from how I had functioned before. I had always expected myself to produce and keep on producing, pushing past exhaustion on a regular basis, skipping meals to get the task at hand done faster. It was as though I, myself, had become the task, and my identity, the product. My real self, my body and soul, had been lost.

So to distinguish myself from "things"—my surroundings, my work, my family seemed strange indeed. Those first few weeks "myself" consisted only of a broken body. I had no real acquaintance with the inner me as yet, so I focused on that body almost as if she was a separate being and I learned to care properly for her.

Taking care of Michael and the children were the only other values I found left in my heart. Everything else melted away and was clearly beyond my capabilities. Even that proved too much for me and I found myself leaning more on Michael to take the leadership role. The first two weeks after my hospital trauma our concerned parishioners brought dinners and saved me from struggling to fight the nausea while preparing food.

Slowly these floating, lost-in-time days slipped past and the physical pains I had suffered somehow began to unravel into a new kind of pain. I had been terrified of the strange changes in my body already, but there was, I sensed, a deeper fear, a terror, and I needed help—I needed someone to help me find this pain and pull it out of my depths before it swallowed all of me forever.

When my physician again suggested I begin talking to a psychologist, I was finally ready for help. It was the beginning of September—just six weeks from that tennis game in July. As I dialed the number of the man she had recommended, I was like a desperate drowning victim, coming up for the third time and gasping for life-giving oxygen. Michael still suspected that all was physical, but I now sensed that there was some sort of a volcano in me. Before it erupted, I wanted to find help. With an appointment scheduled just a couple days away, I sat down to begin a journal. I hadn't written any sort of diary since junior high days, but I had this overwhelming desire to sort out my thoughts and get in touch with this strange person I had become.

So that September 2, 1987, I began to write:

> *I'm on a journey; one I never would have chosen. I gladly would have changed my course had I known my steps led here. But this journey rather chose me, or more accurately, **God** chose this journey **for me**. All I know of Him tells me that this journey is safe; that it is good. It is my knowledge of Him that helps me face each day right now. And not only putting one foot before the other, but looking with wide-open hopeful eyes for His hand as He leads me through.*
>
> *There's no doubt that I will never forget this episode in my life. I'll never be the same person. I didn't know I had so much inside left to break!*
>
> *Out of necessity, I focus on getting well. But over and over again I see the Lord using the boils of my body to touch someone else. I feel sensitized to the pain of others like I've never known. I feel sympathy, and perhaps less fear. My Healer knows what He is about!*

Six days later, after seeing the psychologist, I wrote this:

September 8, 1987

So many days have tumbled by and I feel as though I've come miles in just this week and yet discouraged that nothing has changed.

Last week I met with a psychologist, which is indicative of my total desperation. I thought my chest would constrict to breathlessness on the way there, but as soon as I settled on his proverbial couch (leather, of course, but I sat instead of lying out like a person in analysis!) I began to rattle on as though my life depended on it; I guess because I felt it did. It went well until he looked at his watch, what a letdown! I wasn't ready to stop. It wasn't all better yet! We had hardly scratched the surface! And suddenly it seemed so impersonal—as though I had hung out all my bloody, oozing wounds for him to see and he was too busy to tend to them.

This week has been one of looking back; willingness to lift lids usually kept securely closed. This began when Dr. H. suggested I talk about myself, starting with my earliest memory. As I panned back, I was three again, making myself cinnamon toast and watching television. I would always hold a Kleenex lightly over my nose to breathe because I liked the smell and the sense of security it brought. And I remember my mother leaning over the banister and slurring her words together asking me, "Susan, are you all right?"

I've always known my scars and pain, having accepted them as the necessary ticket to being a sensitive person. My mother had been alcoholic, my younger sister born profoundly retarded and blind, pushing my mother to suffer a nervous breakdown when I was three, leaving me with my grandparents for five years. My father's death when I was sixteen and then my mother's at twenty-three crowned the bloody past. But I had survived. My life with Michael and my children had been so good and I so seemingly whole. How did all the shards of my broken-apart past come together at once to wound me?

I have closed down as much of my life as possible. I gave up my Sunday School class, will not be teaching the women's Bible study, will not take the part-time job I had lined up at the dentist's office, will not be a room-mother at the elementary school, will stop taking Grandma shopping every week, will not lead the women's retreat, will stop hostessing dinners. I'm thankful at this point to be caring for my children, feeding and clothing my family and being a wife to Michael. There is no more I can do now and I'm trying to learn to accept that.

At Dr. H's advice I accompanied my family to the mountains of Maryland for a long-awaited retreat and reunion with our former church family. I thought he was crazy to suggest that I go. In fact, Michael and I decided that it would be a mistake for me to risk the trip. I was always teetering on the edge of panic, especially at the thought of being with people in a potentially stressful setting. I had nothing to lose, we thought, by staying home and much to gain by resting and relaxing. We couldn't have been more wrong! One hour before they were to leave, the panic of being left home alone outscreamed the panic of going. Preferring to suffer in the comforting presence of my family, I felt pulled to go. So one hour until takeoff and I'm throwing clothes into a laundry basket! This from the woman who always carefully plans and co-ordinates clothes a week before a trip and then folds them gently into neat stacks with the matching shoes and jewelry. Never have I prepared for a trip in such a cavalier manner!

As soon as we drove irrevocably down the driveway, I was sure I'd made a terrible mistake. There was no turning back and anxiety welled up like a tidal wave. When we arrived six hours later, I curled up like a wounded caterpillar in our bed and tried to fight the overwhelming, foreign passions and chemicals that claimed my body. No use to recount the numerous joys of my life. No use to realize afresh that I have nothing to fear. Only the grinding, strangling sense of something too terrible to be real coating my insides like a toxic chemical. Michael rescued me with a walk to work off some of the adrenalin. It was there that we saw the first of the Lord's gifts to me that weekend. A lovely doe, so perfect and sweet it seemed unreal, was standing just yards away. She looked so peaceful and I felt as though the Lord was reaching down and giving me His peace.

But the most profound gift came as I braved entry into the throng of people. The adrenalin that had coursed through my body for so long to keep me going at full tilt and to keep my inner pain hidden had burned out my nerve endings. So by then, every bit of stimulation was like electrocution. A little noise, a little stress, brought a reaction as if a 500 pound grisly bear had lurched out from behind a bush. So it took physical courage to leave the sanctuary of my room. But even more frightening was the prospect of being seen the way I now was. They had known me as fearless and strong; now I was frightened and weak. But the Father gave me the grace to venture out.

My fears were overtaken by bone-crushing hugs. With each one I felt more and more infused with their love and acceptance. Some shared their own pain and reached out to ME in need. Most cried with me, either audibly and unashamedly or by the silent pools in their eyes. What a gift that these people should love us so. There is a tie between us stronger than I ever knew. Through these dear tender people God gave me the greatest gift – the gift of hope.

Chapter 7

After returning home, a phone call with a friend brought the rest of my defenses crashing down. It was some kind of a turning point and when I look back it seems as though that day my heart cracked open and years and years of pain were exposed. It was a terrifying feeling and I wanted to stuff it all back inside, but her words to me on the phone that day made me see that this was it; there was no turning back now. What was happening was very real. I had survived my childhood and functioned in my later life by shielding myself from reality with a thick cloak of denial. That denial was second nature to me, learned as it was so early in life. The denial of reality and the faux pictures and twisted beliefs I had constructed were so unquestionably a part of me that I had no sense that I was so entrenched in a false reality.

September 9, 1987

Today I'm feeling shock. I spent an hour on the phone with Mary and am forced to acknowledge the inner sickness that I would so like to deny. It's almost as if I'm afraid that I am a Pandora's Box and if I lift the lid to look and acknowledge, all the most overwhelming, life-threatening horrors will engulf me and there will be no escape.

Mary told me about her physical symptoms when she was so terribly depressed that she was hospitalized for several weeks, and that's what scares me. She really understood my inadequate description, because SHE HAD BEEN THERE TOO! Some measure of comfort there, but oh, so scary. This "thing" is bigger than me and I don't know how to deal with it. I don't want to be swallowed up.

Mary knew what I meant about the chest pain and pressure, she knew exactly what I feel when the "flu-y" feeling comes. She knew the inability to eat and the fear as the weight drops off. She knew the awful anxiety and that feeling of no escape and that desperation to get away. Mary knows, and now I think I know that what is happening is real and it's not just going to go away. There's a life-time of ugly inside trying to get out and I'm afraid. How big is this going to get?

It amazes me how long it took for the layers and layers of denial that I had woven about myself from earliest childhood to come undone. I, myself, had to come undone before the process could even begin because these layers had become the very essence of my being. God had to knock me flat before I could even see there was something lurking there and still I clung to the hope that this was not real and would disappear soon. I thought that if I could plug in the right remedy all would be well.

It was during these early weeks of September that I began to understand why I was being flooded with memories and pain. I really was like a volcano that had been smoking imperceptibly but when life heated up enough, out gushed the carefully tamed but simmering lava I'd always concealed.

God began to pull memories from me by giving me dreams that forced me to look at things I had put away long ago. The dreams and flashbacks that would hit me during the day brought with them intense and painful emotions; emotions that I wasn't accustomed to feeling because somewhere along the line I had learned the trick of numbness in order to survive the pain. Now my emotions had no mercy and would roll over me like a cement truck and leave me with a multitude of physical symptoms in their wake.

Something else interesting began happening—as I looked at my feelings and my emotional pain, the physical pain lessened. As time went on, the more I learned to deal with my feelings and to look at the memories with the Lord, the less plagued I was with physical problems.

September 10, 1987

Last weekend I found hope, but yesterday the first of healing came to me. I spent most of the day crying—it felt as though there was no *bottom. The crying made my chest feel looser. I couldn't wait the whole week before seeing Dr. H. again so I called and went to see him mid-week. The first session I had presented a very together falling-apart person, but today there was no hiding the pain I was feeling. I didn't try to analyze or explain either—I just cried and began to share my fear. It was an odd experience to grope for help, but the understanding he gave was like a balm. I began to share memories that have been locked away all these years; locked away because to remember brought pain accompanied always by guilt. I had sensed it was wrong to feel or show my pain so I had learned to lock it away. The way he listened helped me continue, cautiously monitoring the expression on his face. What I saw reflected back to me was a sympathetic understanding of the pain, the confusion of a little girl trying to endure. Somehow I had grown up thinking it was my reactions to what was happening that was abnormal, that I shouldn't feel the shock, the worry, the fear or horror. It was as though I had no reference point for what was "normal.": I had always understood that what was required of me was NO emotion, NO reaction, other than to reassure those around me that all was well. So I learned to meet trauma with frozenness, and I learned to meet it **alone.***

Dr. H said that my childhood left me with the holes that would always be with me. He said I had spent my life coping in various ways with the gaps; some of these were healthy and successful and others not. In the process of our move here, my coping mechanisms had broken down and life and my pain became overwhelming. I suppressed and fought on in a frenzy until I could suppress no more and now everything was surfacing. There's a frightened little girl within me and I think she never had the time to be a little girl.

As I began to remember and talk about my childhood, so many concepts filtered through to me. Actually, simply the idea that my childhood had been painful and had left lasting scars was novel. While I was growing up it seemed important to appear as though I was unaffected by the trauma around me. I learned early that "negative" emotions such as anger, frustration or fear would only cause more problems for me. And so I learned not only that displaying such feelings would bring trouble but also that *having* them wouldn't do me any good either. The obvious solution was to believe I had the power to control my feelings. I could numb myself to anything negative or too intense. In essence, I learned to filter out the colors of life and to live in a kind of safe gray. The odd thing about this kind of survival maneuver, as I have since discovered, is that as I began to dance this dance of survival, there was nothing cognitive going on inside me. The dance became so much a part of my inner being, that I was unaware of the whole set-up I had put together to mask, numb and control my feelings and reality itself.

Even as I began to open up that carefully "screwed down" coffin lid and risk talking for the first time in my life, I was monitoring the face of the psychologist for any signs of disapproval or disgust. The shame I felt for being who I was penetrated deep into my core and I was looking for his disdain. He was open and gentle; I continued to talk.

Chapter 8

September 12, 1987

The days I crawl through are like a series of ups and downs. And it IS like crawling—every moment seems to require so much effort and being alive feels like something I've never done before.

I think I'm trying too hard to control what's happening to me instead of "letting it happen". It's hard to let go when keeping control is such a habit and what is happening to me feels so strange and frightening. God's spirit reminds me to allow God to work. But often I forget and need many reminders.

Thursday was a wonderful day—strong, no weird "chemical feelings", my chest loose, my stomach fine. But Friday I looked old and haggard again and felt tired—fluy-nervy. Seems as though I should be thankful there are good days now at all, yet instead I feel discouraged and afraid that I am like this.

Last night I was on a crying jag again. My emotions are such a jumbled mess; I don't know WHAT I feel. Nothing is familiar—everything feels like "bizarro world"; like a waking nightmare. I feel desperate to wake up, to escape, but I am awake and there is no escape.

Sleeping was worse—I woke before dawn crying and mumbling. In my dream I was home again in Amberley with my mother, sobbing and shouting at her. I was filled with such a fury, such rage as I spewed it all forth, one hurt after another for her to finally see. All these injuries that

I had worked so hard to convince her, and myself, didn't matter, instead had been collected into a massive ball of pain and stored away.

I don't understand what I'm wading through. Where do these memories come from and why are they pouring forth now? Why do I get better for a few hours and then start the cycle all over again? If anyone I knew were going through this, I would write them off as a lunatic. I feel such a conflict, both needing people and fearing what they do—or might do—to me.

Progress Report:

1. *Beginning to let go of the feeling of responsibility for other's happiness and well-being.*

2. *Losing fear of strong emotions—fear and anger especially. I'm thawing out and finding I can feel without something terrible happening.*

3. *Acknowledging my anger at my parents' lies, cover-ups and neglect, hurting me.*

4. *Acknowledging anger at Mama for leaving me alone, for letting me take care of her instead of allowing me to be the child that I was.*

5. *Acknowledging anger at Daddy for hurting my mother, for scaring and embarrassing me, for keeping our family from BEING a family.*

6. *Admitting when I'm angry!*

7. *Crying—in the past limited to about a bi-annual event, now the flood doesn't seem to want to stop. God gives me space while the kids are in school to crawl in His lap and cry. That helps. I walk the line between*

sharing enough with the kids to keep them from worry or guilty feelings of responsibility, and protecting them from the pain they could not understand or bear. I'm becoming thankful for the openness our current family has been built on and appreciating the un-expectedness of that honesty in light of my own upbringing.

8.   *Seeing how I had lost so much of myself in trying to conform to my idea of who I SHOULD be—all areas perfectly in control, pleasing, teaching, caring, carrying everyone, flawless wife and mother—when it hurt to be stretched so far, when the things that made me "me" were neglected, when I performed out of duty without joy or even the will, thinking I HAD to do it all or I would be bad, selfish, disappointing to the church and my husband, and abandoned.*

9.   *Realizing I've some discovering to do regarding who I am—a sort of delayed adolescence. Am I really this performing wonder, this extrovert? Or am I a person who needs quiet and space? A person who juggles several balls or a person who holds only a few closely? Can I really do everything perfectly if I just try hard enough and do I really want to do everything perfectly??*

10.   *Seeing that God has given me the equipment to get through this tunnel. Friends, loving husband, counselor, doctor, and best and worst of all... time. I dread it taking time. Time means it isn't going away fast. Time means it is going to keep hurting; but time also means a space, a place, a possibility, a beginning, process, growth. God has given me time.*

The whole idea of having to wait out any kind of process, and feeling as though I would-be "caught with my pants down" in the meantime, was tough to accept. My habit was to look critically at what was happening, find the solution, and fix it. As soon as I felt some strength returning, I would take up my usual campaign. I was continually surprised by the layers of hurt within me. This sort of suffering, without the shroud of denial and numbness, was raw. I was still thinking that if I would only avail myself to God's Hand, He would work quickly to put my pieces back together. What I had not yet experienced was the way suffering works patience in the human heart.

September 16, 1987

I'm trying to practice trusting God in small increments, just a few hours at a time. It's been quite a revelation to see that I don't know how to trust. I had thought I knew the Word, but as God peels back the thin onion-like layers of denial and His Spirit tunnels under, I'm beginning to see that I am always on guard. I am always checking my control, making sure I'm ready to catch the person, the situation, always keeping disaster at bay.

Now I have NO control over me or my life. There seems to be no way I can make sure I help God or others work this out. I feel utterly helpless and forced to the test; so afraid of being discarded in weakness. This is walking the highest tightrope without a net.

The audacity of believing I could or even would be called on to help God out rings true for a person drowning under the weight of "being required". Growing up in a home where the adults were absent or out of control created for me an atmosphere and belief system of "requiring". If I didn't come through, who will? To lean into and relax upon another, even God Himself, is unthinkable.

September 17, 1987

Last night I woke at 1:30 AM with grinding stomach pains and my heart pounding. I had been very emotionally caught up in a dream; a double-feature dream that my subconscious ran through twice as though to ensure the message coming through. The second time through the dream was exactly the same except for the addition of some very specific details.

My husband, children and I were in an unfamiliar house when suddenly I was seized with the conviction that we had to be out of that house by 1:00. Michael was skeptical and the children wandering off, so I pleaded with them and struggled to push them out the door. We piled into the car and as we backed down the driveway, at precisely 1:00, the house exploded and fell into ruins. I was filled with relief; we had escaped and it was over.

I woke briefly at that point and pondered the meaning of my dream. What was I so determined to leave? New Jersey? But then, as though my subconscious was resolved that I receive the message, when I fell back into sleep, I dreamed the same dream again, this time with the specific details that helped me understand what I was escaping.

In the rerun it was the same house, the same resistance from Michael and the children, but now I was wandering about the house, noticing the many things I had inherited from my parents. I looked at the oil paintings, I picked up the blue Chinese bowl and for a moment I cradled it in my arms. I knew then that in order to survive, I would have to leave them behind. I had to escape by 1:00, and I saw with dawning clarity that I was better off leaving everything behind. Again, we hurried to the car and, just as it had happened the first time, we backed down the driveway at exactly 1:00 and the house exploded and was gone.

I woke again as though I had been shaken. Is that me struggling to leave something behind before it buries me?

Somewhere inside myself I knew that it was time to uncover the painful memories and dammed up emotions of a little girl. It was time to remember and time to grow up. I had started the process with more desperation and terror than determination. The gun was to my head; I felt I had no choice. Now the understanding that something about my memories of me and my childhood did not ring true began to pierce the superficial layers of denial. The work of navigating more inner layers would come later.

Chapter 9

The memories came back to me, little by little, in bite size increments and I was continually aware that God didn't give me more than I could process. With each remembrance came intense emotional pain and often the whole gamut of physical hindrances that now seemed so familiar. The process was like a series of waves; I would feel anxious, then the memory would surface in a dream or a waking flash-back. With the memory came pain, usually intense fear, and sometimes such heavy sorrow, and occasionally anger. I needed to react to the memory. I found it important to allow room for the feelings that came bursting forth room just to "be". If I didn't allow myself to cry and talk through the memory's pain, I would be swallowed up in physical pain. Years later I would understand at a visceral level the drive of the addict to escape these two unacceptable torture camps: see the horror and feel the searing emotions or be undone by the body's reaction to the stress of burying the truth. Medicating the edge off only serves to compound the body's cry for help.

Seeing Dr. H only once a week meant there were many waves that he was unavailable to take me through. Michael proved a loving listener and I shared the memories with him, but I spent most of my time alone and it was the Lord who listened so faithfully. My crying was sometimes so intense it was more of a wailful moan and I muttered and questioned and pounded my fist and He listened.

Leaving: it seemed as though so many of my memories had to do with people leaving. I remember one night when I was three years old as though I'd stored a video behind my eyes. I had been asleep, it was dark, and my father burst into my room and seized my piggy bank. He was muttering and slurring words that didn't make sense; something about money. He seemed to be asking me something and he seemed so angry.

What had I done? I was afraid and he continued to ask me why it wasn't enough. Hadn't he provided for me? I didn't move, I didn't say anything. Then I heard my mother yelling for him to stop. He left the room but the yelling continued and only heated up. It was a raw screaming and I buried further under the blanket, helpless.

In the morning, the house was quiet as I crept down the stairs. There, at the foot of the stairs, I found my father's tool chest. It was packed and as I looked about me, I saw the disintegration of my life. How could I know at three that this tool chest was a symbol of dramatic change? Yet somehow I knew, and those packed boxes around me confirmed my worst fear. Someone was leaving.

There's an instant of anguish, then a tremendous black hole in the picture. I remember so clearly what led up to our separation, and then I remember nothing. My mother was taken to a psychiatric hospital because her drinking had rendered her unable to function and I suspect she may have been suicidal as well. Though the photo albums show good times, my earliest memories of her are clouded with slurred words and taking care of myself. My father took an apartment somewhere near the hospital and I was taken to my grandparents' home. My sister, Annie, was taken to an institution and now the leaving was complete.

Annie. Annie was my ally, my buddy, and in some ways my charge. I don't remember being aware that there was anything different about Ann. She had been born just thirteen months after me and three months premature. Considering the technology of the 50's, it's quite a miracle that she survived at all. The massive dosage of oxygen used in the incubator had burned her eyes and she was completely blind. Instead of colored irises with the black dot of a pupil, she has milky irises with no visible pupil at all.

While Ann was a baby, the mental retardation was undetected. My mother was determined to overcome the blindness by introducing her to the world of sound. She bought toys that made noises, played music for her in the hope of helping her compensate for her blindness. But as the months wore on, it became evident that something else was wrong with Annie. She didn't advance to new stages the way a normal child would. She took a long time to learn to sit up, to crawl, to walk. As the truth about her second child became undeniable, my mother was less and less able to face the painful reality. She found escape in alcohol. There in that fuzzy world, she didn't have to cope.

But to my toddler's mind, Annie was my best playmate. Every morning, I would climb into her crib and it was giggle time. I loved to make her laugh! Later, when she learned to talk, she would repeat everything I said back to me. Or sometimes she would suddenly come out with some word or phrase from some other long forgotten conversation. Our favorite mode of conversation was song; I would sing to her in my non-musical and usually off-key voice while she would cock her head to the side and listen very carefully. Then she would sing the song back to me, but this time it would be on-key and note perfect. This was our own special way of communicating and it bound us together in a sisterhood that closed everyone else out.

I have no memory at all, though, of our being torn apart. No recollection of how it happened or what I felt; in fact, no memory of anything for perhaps a year. As though I was in shock, my mind froze over and wiped the slate clean. Years after my breakdown, my aunt told me of how I was the little girl no one knew quite how to help. I was throwing up regularly and crying like an abandoned child. I don't remember that period.

My memories click back into focus when I was five and had settled into life with my grandparents. I remember friends and birthday parties. I have a keen picture of my grandmother making May baskets with me and sending me out to deliver them by hooking them onto the doorknob, ringing the bell and running away with giddy delight. There were the holidays when she would strew candy on the floor and claim the Easter Bunny had just run through or Santa had appeared.

I also remember my nighttime terrors and facing a long, dark hall in order to run to her and climb into her bed. I don't remember her ever chastising me for that invasion or refusing me. My grandfather was a quiet sort of man; a product of his generation. He seldom showed his emotions and played the hen-pecked husband role, led impatiently by his wife up to a point and then standing his ground. But he encouraged me to read to him every night and plant seeds of my own in his beautiful garden. Those seeds took hold in my heart too and grew into a deep passion for creating in the soil. This was a period of peace for me, safety and calm that I had never before experienced.

When I was eight, this would all be ripped away from me. My happy memories there would be replaced with forgetfulness or disdain toward those loving grandparents in order to support my mother's fragile mental health. She needed constant reassurance that she was not a bad mother, that I did not miss my grandparents, that I loved only her. So I put away that happy time somewhere deep where it was no longer accessible. And at eight I was immersed in a new hell while trying to maintain the picture of the happy family that had gotten back together.

Chapter 10

September 19, 1987

The good days are beginning to out-number the bad days. It's been hard to miss so much of life; I stayed home from church last Sunday and the Ladies Fall Tea went on without me, but this cocoon of space around me feels good. I'm riding a precarious surf board over the waves of memories that swell up and carry me raging along, then ebb and dip. It takes concentration to stay upright.

Some friends came over Thursday night to share their own painful journey with me. He had suffered his own physical and emotional break-down just a few years ago and I was hoping to feel less alone and peculiar by hearing of his experience. It was helpful to share the pain and get to know them on a deeper level, but not quite the life-ring I hoped it would be. We are all so different and our path as pilgrims through these trials is one so unique that I think the ultimate aloneness is inescapable. What I need to grasp fully is who walks with me and the sufficiency of His presence.

Today while reading Matthew, I was struck by a familiar passage:

"Come to me all you who are weary and burdened and I will give you rest. Take my yoke upon you and learn from me, for I am gentle and humble in heart, and you will find rest for your souls. For my yoke is easy and my burden is light."

It seems as though, in some sense, I have strapped myself to a heavy cart, worn the yoke meant for a whole team of dumb oxen and envisioned

*Christ merely **in** my cart, cheering me on as I pulled Him along. God forgive me for my pride.*

September 23, 1987

I feel such terror. The world seems like a huge gaping space, no walls, no boundaries. My life has become the ride at the amusement park that whips one around with such force that bodies are plastered against the walls while the bottom drops out from under the riders. The bottom has dropped out of my world, and there seems no escape from this ride.

September 29, 1987

Days like today make me desperate. I hurt and there seems no comfort for it. My mind is a befuddled jumble and I'm crawling through this disconnected sort of land. And I'm so terribly tired. Today I feel too tired to keep going, but the awful part of this tired is that there is no choice, no escape.

Meeting with Dr. H made me more unglued today. I'm not sure why. He did, in a sense, confront me with myself by telling me that I am a "hyper-active person", someone who is always vigilant of her surroundings. He said my antennae were up and I was constantly bombarded with stimuli that I was unable to distinguish as important or to be ignored. He's right. That's where my keen ability to "read" people comes from, my "vibes". Somehow the thought of myself as nervous or hyper-active was repulsive and I was so scared to think of myself this way.

After seeing Dr. H I drove to Andi's house like "a horse to the barn"—under the pain there is a joy in what unfolds in our relationship. To be able to feel like a disintegrating maggot-covered mess and be loved and hugged is a new joy. Michael's presence continues to be a source of strength and stability for me too. How ever would a person go through this alone? Sometimes I can so clearly see the Lord, but other

days there is no center, no focus apart from people who love me leading
me to Him.

Slowly, as the days of fall labored by, the Lord was revealing to me a secret compartment, filed away long ago and simply labeled: My Childhood. Never explored, no questions asked and emotions frozen. As I began to remember, I had a million questions and now no one to ask. Every strange or terrifying happening had been met with acceptance—this was how it was. There was no freedom to explore the hows and the whys; survival is what was called for, always. I know there were times when I questioned and looked for attention at the beginning; after five years at my grandparents where I had adjusted and found a place carved out for me in which I could feel comfortable, I was whisked away again by my reuniting parents. I was eight years old.

At first I seem to have expected certain attentions and the care that I had grown to consider normal. I remember asking my father to spend time with me, but he was preoccupied with his sales records or boat-building in the evenings and week-ends. When he was home, he was drinking constantly. I can't remember seeing him at home without a can of beer in his hand. My mother was hanging by a thread as she struggled to make this new life work and overcome her alcoholism. She was gone most evenings to AA meetings. There were week-end conferences and she went back to work as a nurse. I so distinctly remember their faces which scolded, "Susan, how could you ask for that? How could you say that?" If I questioned or went against the tide in any way or looked for attention, the disapproval and shock they gave back were more than my shaky childish ego could stand.

So I learned, as children do, to understand the unwritten and even unspoken family rules that would keep peace. Don't ask, don't express negative feelings like anger or fear, don't expect or ask for attention, and don't react when something strange or frightening happens. DON'T ROCK THE BOAT`!

Keeping to the rules, though, didn't do much for the pain and turmoil I was feeling inside. I didn't cry. I never told anyone my fear or pain; instead the panic manifested itself in physical ways. As a three year old at my grandparents' house, I vomited when the submerged anxiety became too much. As a second grader, newly reunited with my parents, I experienced trepidation and panic at school. I dreaded walking to the gym where we had lunch every day;

somehow sitting at those crowded lunch tables terrified me and my throat would close up so that eating was nauseating.

The world was too frightening, too big for me, and because I couldn't tell anyone and there seemed no one to help, I was panicking. The school contacted my parents and arranged a meeting with the school counselor where I can't remember being too communicative. What did help me was the counselor's suggestion that my mother meet me for lunch for a period of time. I'll never forget the relief when the lunch bell rang each day and I tore out the door looking with desperation for her blue Fairlane parked outside. I wonder what would have happened to me if she hadn't taken that time to lunch with me. After lunch, I was fortified and confident to face the afternoon and this special attention and affirmation eased some of my fears.

While life at home didn't improve, the natural resiliency of childhood helped me adjust. As I learned the "rules" I was more and more able to protect myself from some of the pain.

My father's drinking continued to escalate and I accepted as normal for him that he would spend every evening hunched over his desk, drinking can after can of beer, completing his sales records for the day to the drone of the television in the background. I learned not to bother him and later in the evening, when the beer had changed this man, I learned to stay out of his way. After hours of drinking, there were usually two ways he might behave. There was the angry, yelling, out of control Daddy and there was the staggering, silly Daddy that said things I didn't understand but that scared me somehow and didn't seem right.

Nothing at home was safe and predictable. My father was totally unreliable and my mother oscillated between strong, loving attention and sudden irrational craziness. One day she locked me outside and I could hear her laughing on the other side of the door. Terrified, I pounded the door and begged to be admitted. When I threw up on the porch, she opened the door but I still remember feeling it was I who had done something wrong.

All my mother's strength was consumed by constantly covering for my father. He continued to get up every morning and go to work, no matter what had transpired the previous night. But every evening and weekend he was out of control. Some evenings he didn't come home until the morning hours and many times he left for errands but never made it past the local bar.

Because he was so drunk at home, dramatic and frightening things were always happening. It was normal for sudden and scary things to occur. Once I heard my mother screaming followed by the slam of the back door. Racing to the window I saw her running with a broom into what appeared to be a wall of flames. My father had thrown gasoline into the incinerator and ignited the whole back yard. I thought I would again lose both of them, but the fire was at last beaten into oblivion and no one was hurt. No one ever mentioned the fire.

Another time Daddy was in the garage working on the boat he was building. He spent every weekend meticulously piecing together a 22 foot sailboat from scratch, each mahogany and teak part perfection itself. His six-pack of beer kept him constant company as he dreamed of sailing. This time he was working on a burner in the garage and too drunk to be careful. From the attached house, we heard the explosion. He escaped with only some painful burns This, too, we never talked about.

One of the most frightening memories was being left home alone when I was eight or nine and no one came home as dark approached. It was a Saturday and my mother was gone for the day leaving my father in charge. He was, as expected, working on the boat and I occupied myself. Sometime during the day, my father said he was going to have the keel poured. I wasn't invited and he left. The day wore on and I remember sitting on the floor of my room playing and then suddenly noticing that it was dark. I was alone in the house and it was ink black everywhere except my room. No one had come home. Where were they? I can still feel the little- girl- raw -fear as I crept from my room, heart pounding, groping for lights as I went. I made it as far as the telephone in my parents' room and called my best friend who lived a block up the street. There was some relief knowing she would meet me in the street, but still I had to face all those pitch black stairs leading down into an even darker living room. Then the front door and the still blacker street. We lived in a rural part of Illinois with dirt roads and no street lights to break apart the darkness.

I don't remember when my parents came home or even how they found me at my friend's house. What I do recall was hearing the horrible screaming between my parents about the event and feeling, again, that somehow I was to blame. It was my fault that my mother was so angry at my daddy.

It was during this time that I began to have a recurring nightmare. It was one of those dreams that seems so perfectly real, each detail precise and presented by the subconscious in lifelike color. At each recurrence, I would wake with pounding heart and screams frozen in my throat.

In the nightmare, I am alone in the house, shrouded in darkness, standing in the living room by the window. Outside, the sky is black except for the horizon, where bands of red and gold blazed across and met the dark. I see the dark shadow of a figure moving swiftly away through the dark, silhouetted against the fiery backdrop. It is my mother and she is carrying a suitcase and I know instantly that she is leaving. After a moment of panic, I take comfort in remembering that at least Daddy is still with me. I am not alone. But just as soon as I remember his presence, a huge hairy spider comes lumbering out of the garage, Daddy's workshop, and I know with childlike dread that the enormous eight-legged creature has eaten my father and I am now completely alone. Then in my dream I begin screaming with every fiber of my being and that's when I would wake. This dream was to haunt me over and over again for many years but as a little girl, I never told anyone.

Chapter 11

October 11, 1987

Today the mail brought me a book about alcoholic families from my aunt. She said I should particularly read the chapter on family roles because she saw me playing the "hero role" as I was growing up. She said I was a little girl who tried so hard to be good, who tried to make everyone happy and everyone else look good. I could see immediately that she was right; the role fit perfectly. I'm beginning to see, too that the way alcoholism touched my life—touched?? More like devoured!—greatly affected me and the person I have become. This is something I need to look at closely and unflinchingly.

I'm nestled up in the corner of the couch and from this vantage point, I can see my cherry tree just outside the window. I love this tree; I've always loved weeping cherry trees that arch their arms so gracefully out over their solid trunk and sweep the ground with their fingers. When Michael bought me this little tree, it was only about four feet tall but the root ball was about the same in diameter! He lovingly labored, digging the biggest hole I'd ever seen to plant it for me, making this tree doubly precious. Today the bending limbs are getting bare and the stubborn leaves that cling are yellowed and dying. It's hard to imagine that this spring it will be dressed in glorious pink finery.

*In a way, this tree is a reminder of my hope. **Perhaps when my cherry tree blooms this spring, I'll be whole.***

Weeping cherry trees remained a reminder and a symbol to me from that day forward. Every new home and every new garden just had to have one in the landscape as a symbol of hope; a declaration of the powerful presence of my God and His healing that was almost unimaginable to me at that time when I was curled in the sofa corner in 1987.

October 27, 1987

I'm struggling to live in the NOW—to enjoy today and live it fully. I've missed so much of my life by spending it organizing and preparing for the future. This is probably the hardest for me. I'm a great escaper of the present. I'll do it better, make it better, live it better, feel better, look better, etc. etc. Slowing down helps me focus on today. Keeping plans for the future down to a minimum helps too right now. And consciously "feeling" today—all of it—while enjoying and expressing those varied feelings instead of being numb.

I'm still confused about the gut level insecurity I feel, masking it with varying degrees of success. And I puzzle over its manifestation in compulsivity and over-driven-ness. It comes upon me so stealthily and when I'm in the midst of it, I find it hard to stop. Before I know it, I'm fussing to make everything come out orderly and trying to control every aspect of life around me. I feel so responsible to make everyone and everything about me safe, solid, happy, lined up and correct. Something new and helpful has been letting others, especially the children, be responsible for themselves as much as possible. I can do this by making concrete parameters with concrete consequences. Then, not only do they know THEIR boundaries, but I know MINE!

November 4, 1987

I think I've strayed from writing because I have no idea how I'm doing. The last couple days I've felt afraid again and had the various gamut of physical symptoms from the night-time nerve problems to the stomach cramps. Yesterday I felt quite depressed and wished there was someone to just hold my hand. But, I survived the day and was very glad when the family started arriving home and filling the airspace with the usual racket and chaos.

Today I went errand-running—not very confidently—and then played racquet ball with Michael at lunch. This was the first time since June and I wasn't sure what to expect. We didn't play particularly hard or long, but considering I had no wind or speed at all, I didn't play too badly! The exercise left me feeling refreshed and more like my old self and it was fun to feel "fun" again.

I've divided up responsibilities for Thanksgiving among the family so that all are contributing one part to the meal. I feel that passing on some of the responsibility has broken me out of shackles and I may really enjoy the day much more.

Fall feels like a gift from the Lord. I'm enjoying the swirling colorful leaves crunching under my shoes on my walks, and the whole changing landscape as though for the first time. Maybe it's so beautiful this year because last year I didn't notice as I was rushing through life with a stone in my heart and a thousand yokes on my back. Or maybe because I'm so thankful that dreadful summer is over. Or maybe because I'm coming alive after this wrenching death experience of the last few months.

Sometimes during that fall, I began referring to the fear and pain I felt as "the dragon." The feelings that revealed themselves and pushed and pulled at me seemed life- like and as solid and tangible as a great spike-toed, fire-breathing, slimy-skinned beast. For a long time I was a bit unclear about just what this "dragon" represented to me, but I was sure something was pressing me and threatening to hurt me. If the beast should overcome me, I would be completely undone.

November 7, 1987

It's been a couple tough days since my euphoric Wednesday after-noon. Thursday and Friday were filled with panic, stomach cramps and more panic. My chest tightened into the original knot and I was filled with floating anxieties and those chemical feelings again. Today is better—the dragon is mostly outside the door; just the tip of his tail left to remind me of his presence.

A new feeling keeps overcoming me this past week—one of tremendous longing. I can't figure where it comes from. It's very strong but nameless and hence unfillable.

I need to find my balanced schedule again. I haven't given up walking altogether or writing or Bible study and meditation, but the days are jerks and stops and jumbled disorder. I'm unable to find a comfortable pace of living because I'm so unpredictable. When I'm better for a week at a time, then I'm ready for people, adventure and household tasks. When panic strikes and memories roll, I become hyper-sensitive to everything and need the quiet days on the couch. Some balanced regularity would sure be nice!

When I saw Dr. H, he described this sense of carrying around a deep, dark pit that is common for survivors of troubled pasts. I sat there, totally incredulous as he described the very feeling I have always had and yet found difficult to put into words. I felt like a marooned islander, rescued and returned to the mainland. There were others that knew about that black hole and some of my sense of aloneness dissipated. He said I was in the process of facing what dwelled in that slimy pit—those being my memories, pain and fears that I put away as a little girl. He said I would go through them and pull them out and when I finished, I would see that all that remained in the hole, lurking in the blackness, was fear. As I meditate on this, I feel ready for the process because I know that Jesus holds my hand, goes before me and behind me. He is the great conqueror of fear: "The Lord is my light and my salvation. Whom shall I fear? The Lord is the stronghold of my life, Of whom shall I be afraid?"

November 16, 1987

Try as I might to slow life's pace, the days roar in and tumble past me faster than I can control. The kids were home last Thursday and Friday, then we had Michael's birthday celebration so I cooked up a feast complete with a three layer cake. The weekend was full of keeping up with the kids' activities. By Sunday I had reached the end so I stayed in bed and slept until noon while everyone else went to church. Such unheard of indulgence! There is still guilt when I cannot keep going— still so hard to admit that I "can't".

Today, Monday, I'm still tired and sick of my chest constricting. I think the dragon is trying to chew his way through the door.

November 17, 1987

Values! Before, beauty, things, order and perfection were like shining mysteries that promised so much. I've explored that elusive glitter enough to know that they are only lovely but elusive sequins never worthy of their exalted place. How little they matter now!

My values have shifted as I've matured in the Lord and yet old habits keep pushing me back into familiar ruts. When I'm afraid, the pretty things, the order, the need to control become not just attractive but paramount to survival.

I valued "boxwood garden living"; a life in one of those perfect English gardens with fragrant boxwood hedges precisely clipped and controlled, lining the orderly, crushed shell walkways. God, though has been teaching me the value of pain and the reality of brokenness. It is no wonder it took so much energy and gave me so much frustration to make life line up. It cannot be done! It seems that so much of my need to get the exterior world in control was generated by my need to get the INTERIOR in order. Instead, all that effort made towards boxwood gardens gave only false order and the illusion of security.

My physical symptoms refuse to leave me, as if they know I cannot be trusted: that if I felt normal, I'd only stuff all this back inside and go on as before. My chest has a life of its own now, my stomach continues to play its tricks. The anxiety is usually fleeting and less intense, but always nearby.

But I have more energy now, racquetball once a week and 30-40 minutes of walking every day. My weight has come up and leveled off and my clothes fit again. My blood pressure still fluctuates but stays close to normal limits. I've stopped waking early morning with those awful hyper-tingly feelings. My worst time is still around four every afternoon; a slithering fear floats in and slips around my neck.

November 25, 1987

I'm starting to understand that all my life I played the supporting caretaker role for my parents. I carefully screened my emotions, playing the ever-good girl. I felt so guilty if there was anything going wrong.

I dreamed another one of those graphic dreams last night and this one was full of that condemning guilt. I was in an arena in a prison, surrounded by faceless people. My father stood there in the middle with me, so real and so much himself that it hardly seemed a dream at all. He was accusing me of not trying to be closer to him, saying that it was my fault the relationship had not been right; that I had neglected him. All the faceless people stood accusing me too. I felt overwhelming guilt and shame.

Slowly the shame melted into anger. I turned to fully face my father and I said, clearly, boldly, "How could I get close to you? You were either drunk or on the boat!" All the people let out a sharp intake of breath in sympathetic surprise and then my father faded away. When I woke, I felt clean. The truth was out and the shame was gone.

I'm seeing so many things about myself for the first time. My life-long determination for a fairy-tale world, a boxwood garden, came from a raging need to make everything all right. My life's role of emotionally supporting my parents brought me my self-esteem and sense of usefulness and belonging. If I was very, very good, they wouldn't leave me. If I made myself indispensable, I would have a place where I belonged. I felt guilty that my home was shattered, my parents were broken and suffering. Being "good", achieving, carrying their hurts, seemed to help, so my striving was reinforced.

Emotionally supporting my parents required that my own emotions be carefully and constantly monitored. Only helpful, encouraging feelings and expressions of those feelings were allowed. Anything negative might hurt or drive my parents away; too big a risk for me. This made for an insecure, tenuous relationship where rejection loomed imminent. I learned automatic controls for my emotions, living in the "gray" without the broad spectrum of feelings. After thinking of myself all those years as an even-keeled and unemotional person, what a shock to discover this hidden deeply feeling person that I am.

November 29, 1987

Thanksgiving was lovely! Wednesday night I was feeling shaky but I went to the service and so enjoyed being with the people. Thanksgiving Day was quite unique. Michael got up at 6:30 AM to stuff and enthrone the bird in the oven while I languished in bed. He then squirreled back under the covers and we didn't rise until 10! Our friend John joined us at about 1:00 and I continued to be relaxed—so relaxed that I forgot the cranberries! I'm the person who gives dinner parties from complicated, detailed notes—I do NOT forget the condiment! Michael looked harassed as he struggled with the gravy and I did feel some guilt pangs, but mostly I was thankful. The children each contributed their special dish to the meal, John brought the wine and when we feasted, the feeling of family sharing settled over us like a soft blanket. And, thank you God, I forgot the cranberries!

I'm waiting for a black and white break from the dragon's clutches; a definite release. Instead, it seems more of a gradual overcoming.

November 30, 1987

Dragons, dragons and more dragons. They are breathing fire at my door and I'm leaning hard. I see changes—I'm aware of the emotions that tease me, and for once, I'm not running.

I feel as though I have been so thoroughly broken, shown to be but a vapor. It is as though God gave me a loving swipe across the face, sent me sprawling and said to me, "My child, stop striving. I am God."

December 1, 1987

I finished reading Job this morning and as Job was repenting of his pride and arrogance, I couldn't help but cry over mine. The girl with no limits, strong enough to help everyone else, so definite and self-controlled, was a proud lady. Weakness was for cowards. Brokenness was to be overcome and determined away. I pray these are healing tears.

The book I'm currently reading states that anxiety needs to be dealt with by praising God for the future. This is becoming a new tool for anxious moments and reminds me to focus my thoughts and renew my trust in the Lord.

December 2, 1987

Today is one of those really good days and I'm trying to savor every moment. How I do appreciate the good moments! Circumstantially, the day is a disaster—two kids home with two different kinds of flu, the toilet died and the bathroom downstairs is all torn up—AGAIN—and I'm tired because we didn't go to sleep until after midnight and the therapy group I attended last night was awful. But I feel so much better.

I hesitate to think this because I don't rule out slipping back, even to the brokenness of last summer. (Nothing surprises me anymore!) But there seems to be a real tangible healing within me. SOMETHING is different!

The group leader last night handed out band-aids and the other people seemed miles back, yet had been in therapy longer than I. The counselor had nothing to give but coping mechanisms and what I want is to dig out the "cancer" and be healed. There was much venting of anger, whining and complaining.

I am so grateful that I belong to God, that Jesus has held my hand throughout this painful journey and that the Holy Spirit has been my main counselor. The Spirit of God is the best teacher I could ever have and He has WANTED to impart wisdom to me, has met me faithfully every day and is leading me out of the mire.

At this point in my recovery, the psychologist I was seeing determined that group therapy would be most beneficial for me. I was frightened by the thought of exploring my pain with strangers and exposing myself to others, but my desire for healing won out. By the night of the initial group meeting, I was eager to attend and see what God would do. I was discovering a new longing for "connected-ness" with other people and Dr. H. assured me the people attending were all in some sort of transition in their life. The session was to be directed by a counselor unknown to me.

Though I was disappointed in the group and later determined God was calling me to another path, the meeting did point out to me the treasure I have in the Holy Spirit. He had been leading me in the way of truth all along and my heart was anxious to journey on. I saw, too, that the concept of growing through the pain in a group situation was a good one and that prepared me for what was to come.

Because I had been forced to deal with my childhood traumas alone, with only the resources of a confused and frightened child, being alone has always been my darkest fear. Being ripped from the volatile home and from my unpredictable parents at the tender and vulnerable age of three left a heavy mark. The most difficult part of this journey was not the physical pains or the work of sifting through the wreckage; the hardest part was the inevitable *aloneness* of the path. No other human being was so connected with me as to feel the horror, the despair, the awful grinding fear of facing up to this past, facing up to *me!*

Chapter 12

December 3, 1987

This morning I was flipping through a book on hope for the alcoholic family and suddenly realized I was really hurting. I was overcome with feeling that I had failed—as hard as I had tried to be good, I had lost both my mother and my father. I couldn't help them, I couldn't make it better. Tremendous guilt, tremendous sadness. I don't want to accept that they are gone and our family will never "get better."

Thirty-five years old, both my parents dead for many years and still the weight of responsibility for their welfare hung on my shoulders. How amazing and how odd the dynamic of role reversal is in such a family. To fail to rescue the family brings shame; the core feelings and belief that I not only failed, but I am a failure.

December 13, 1987

I had another one of those dreams. There were no people in this dream except me, creating an eerie aloneness that was frightening. I was at the home of my aunt and uncle, where I stayed for four months when I was six while my grandmother went to Europe. Someone in the dream had told me I had to clean up the bathroom which was a dark, wet mess, towels and clothing strewn everywhere. Everything was covered with slimy filth and as I surveyed the room, I was feeling very small and helpless. The job was too big for me; I just couldn't face it. The feeling of longing and homesickness overcame me as I stood in the dream's doorway, but I couldn't remember for which home I was pining. Suddenly, I realized that I was grown-up and not a little girl anymore. Where was Michael? Why didn't anyone come for me? I felt forgotten and afraid.

These dreams conjuring up old situations and feelings keep coming at regular intervals. It seems that as soon as I dream and analyze my memories, another dream fills my sleeping. These dreams seem different from my usual fare; these are sharp, clearly defined with pointed messages from my sub-conscious. I usually wake suddenly as they all come to some sort of a dramatic conclusion instead of merely fading away. I remember them easily and marvel at the clever way my mind is speaking to me. It seems as though the Lord is using this mode to enable me to see and face the pain I have stored so deeply.

December 15, 1987

Today I was retested for diabetes and I passed! There is now no sign of a sugar problem. My blood pressure was 130/70, even in the setting of the doctor's office. So much healing has taken place!

I'm not running anymore; I'm facing my past and my pain instead of burying myself in activity and order. But what do I replace it with? I take peeks at the black hole, but I'm not sure what to do with it yet. I get waves of aloneness, but don't know where to turn with my dependency. Every encounter with people is a struggle to be calm, to be myself, to believe I have worth. I'm finding I don't know <u>how</u> to live without running.

The hardest part about refusing to run anymore, simply *stopping*, is the sense of feeling as though I have landed abruptly on the edge of a precipice, peering down into the abyss, completely unbalanced. Without the running to avoid the feelings of pain and inadequacy, there is just pain. Until the core feelings of shame and the whole orientation to other people and the world begins to change, there can seem to be no balm to help. This is where the real work of learning to turn to the only One who has the answers begins.

December 16, 1987

Feeling more balanced out today. Last night I attended another group therapy meeting and came at last to a decision. It seems more and more apparent that the leader is not going to be very helpful and that, because the people in the group aren't committed to Christ and His Word, we are poles apart. I do see the merit in group settings so I'm planning to get involved with a Christian counselor-led Adult Children of Alcoholics group. For some time now I've been seeking the Lord's guidance because I was feeling a bit lost at sea. Somehow it seemed time to move forward but which direction? Dr. H. helped me so much those early months. I was like a broken clock; the mainspring had come undone. He gently took the clock apart, piece by piece and set those broken parts side by side on the table. We picked up the shattered components one by one and examined the many angles. Now the clock is piecemeal but I sense he cannot help me reassemble the parts. While I was praying for wisdom, a flyer from this newly formed Christian ACOA group found its way to Michael's desk at church.

I'm beginning to see that my parents' drinking left a mark on me. The hero role I played and my abandonment are my dragons, my dark holes. I'm not sure how much effect their alcoholism had on me, but I'm willing to look.

Over and over again, the same truths, the same lessons made their mark. I had earlier merely glimpsed the effect my childhood had levied on me, and yet the idea would dawn on me repeatedly until at last I understood at my core. The layers of denial in place for all my life had been there to protect me from the knowledge that my parents couldn't parent me. That piece of information is too poisonous for a child to bear. If my parent's behavior can harm me then I, as a helpless child, am in jeopardy. I take the view that it is not them but myself who is flawed and then I hang onto that erroneous belief as though my life depends on it, because it does! Then the fear of abandonment takes up company with the endless need to assure my parents of their wholeness and my own acceptance of their behavior to insure that I will not be left. This world view is set in concrete. It takes time and jack hammering to break it apart.

Everything I learned was like that; I seemed to keep coming back again and again to the very same lessons and one day in frustration, I told Dr. H. that I wasn't getting anywhere. He encouraged me to see that the growing I was doing was like circling a tree; I would move around and around that massive trunk, coming back time and time again to the same side, but if I looked down, I would see that while I was moving *around,* I was also being propelled upward. Now I was indeed several feet off the ground and though the growth seemed repetitive, progress *was* being made. Many times of discouragement later, I would recall his words.

December 20, 1897

It's Sunday morning and I leave for church in a few minutes. How differently I feel now about facing driving to church alone than just a couple months ago! It's good to see and count the progress.

Thoughts are beginning to come together for me. I see more and more clearly what a frightened person I am—what a frightened little girl I was. I think I've put my hand down into that dark hole and found it filled only with fear. I'm no longer a stranger to this feeling of fear that I ran from all my life. So much of the power of that dark hole seems now impotent. Greater is He that is within me.

*The biggest change for me seems to be that I no longer have to **fight** the fear. It seems as though I grew up fighting fear because there was no one there to help me and I had to prove to everyone that I was undamaged goods; nothing and no one had hurt me so don't feel guilty and please don't leave me! If I had admitted the fear, then I would have had to deal with something bigger than I, alone. Feeling so responsible for all my parents' struggles made me strive to assure them that I was unaffected by all the pain around me. Such energy was required to maintain the lie! It was a life-long battle of pushing a boulder uphill until I tripped and that rock ran me over.*

That fear of being abandoned can set up a lifetime commitment to being "good enough" to earn care and attention. Coupled with the shame learned when "good enough" never really *was*, that fear seems to be assuaged only by trying harder. These are the seeds of perfectionism. Of course, perfectionism is a losing battle because I am not perfect. I am broken. If I could achieve the golden perfect, Christ would have had no need to die for me. But in a family like this, it doesn't feel OK to be anything less than perfect.

All that striving to somehow measure up is exhausting and depressing work. It separated me from everyone else as I kept my mask tightly in place, knowing that if anyone gets a glimpse of what is *really* underneath, I would get rejected. And so the boulder is forever being pushed up that steep incline.

December 22, 1987

Last night I dreamed I was surveying the garden and was dismayed to find rocks everywhere. I couldn't figure out the old pattern or find the plantings that had always been there. Nearby, there was some sort of a root cellar and as I approached the door, I knew there was something frightening and foreboding down there. I had to go down there to do laundry; to make things clean, but I was afraid.

The whole feeling of the dream was that things weren't the way they used to be, the old patterns didn't fit and where did all those rocks come from? There was something scary deep down, hidden away, but I had to face it to become clean.

January 5, 1988

The children are finally back in school after two long weeks. The constant tension and stimuli, not to mention <u>mess</u>, was getting to the unbearable point. We did have some very special times together and for the most part, I managed to let things go so I could enjoy their company.

I continue to be in a hurry to put the pieces of my life back together. I continue to feel as though my clothing has fallen around my ankles and I'd better pull it up fast!

One thing is sure—I can no longer "stuff it". Even if I try, my chest constricts. Maybe I'll become more transparent.

A couple nights in a row, I dreamed of losing things. One night it was my shoes and I was wandering about unable to go out and buy another pair because I was barefoot, cold and exposed. Then it was my jacket I had lost. I'm feeling vulnerable and facing up to my losses.

One of the hardest things about recovery is that it is a *process*. If only swallowing a pill or reciting some mantra, some Bible verse, could catapult us into the category of "healed". It is the day-to-day, grueling *process* of recovery that bogs us down. Part of the battle has to do with the lure of perfectionism and the pain of being seen coming apart. It is a lot easier to admit shortcomings when we can quickly add just how much God has healed us in that area already! We want to cover-up, get there, be finished. Little do we know that it is really in the very un-covered-ness that we begin the healing path. It is only in fully surrendering ourselves to Christ, our broken and wanting selves falling at His feet, needing His mercy beyond all else, that wholeness finds us.

Another difficulty in the word *process* is that life goes on even when we are falling apart. If we could just get off the treadmill long enough to work uninterrupted on our recovery, if the pressures of everyday living would just go away.....But most of us face up to these things while juggling families, homes and jobs. No wonder we are anxious to get it over with! Ah, but that too is a somewhat unwelcome truth: The *process* of recovery is really a life-long journey. It is not that we stay so unglued the rest of our lives. We can do the work and find our balance and joy. But that old siren of perfection that keeps calling us is only vapor. We are not in the *process* to be perfect; we are on God's drawing board to become more and more like Christ so that we may enjoy and serve God better. Better, not perfectly!

Chapter 13

My first encounter with the Adult Children Of Alcoholics group was an emotional one. We were six women, strangers to one another, seated on folding chairs in a small circle in a church basement. Two counselors, Susanne and Richard, were seated in our circle with us. Though it was obvious that we were all nervous, there was an eagerness about the group. After a short introduction, we were asked to give our name and state which of our parents were alcoholic. One by one, the women complied. It was my turn; their eyes looked at me and suddenly I burst into tears. Immediately they reached out with compassion and "Kleenex" and when I finally composed myself, I choked out the words, "My name is Susan and **both** my parents were alcoholics." I cried, I told them, because it was overwhelming to be sharing this information and this pain with others. I wasn't alone and I was glad to be with them.

Embarrassed! I'd never cried in a group like that. Who would have thought the first to cry would be me? The dynamics of the group changed, though, at that moment. We were knit together in the comradeship of support and an openness was born that was undoubtedly a new experience for all of us.

Every Saturday morning I drove to my group meeting and at the same time I began counseling once a week with Susanne. The real work of my recovery had begun!

We spent group time talking about our families, our perceptions, our memories, our roles. For a long time, we each found discussing family stories very difficult. We noticed that we each used some sort of defense mechanism to play down any trauma. Our favorite phrase was, "But it wasn't *that* bad!" One woman described her mother chasing her with an axe and then finished her story with that favorite phrase. Another ploy was to divert attention from ourselves to another: "My father would pass out every night, but that was nothing like what *you* suffered. You must have felt scared!" Mostly, though, we felt guilty because we were telling the family secrets. Each of us had grown up with the unwritten but sacred gag rule. Never telling anyone created isolation and confusion over what is really normal.

At first I don't think we could understand why we were feeling such sadness. We had lived with these family facts all our lives, yet as we began to talk and look at them, we were like a gathering at a funeral home, peering into the casket of our loved one. Except the body lying within had our own face. Slowly we began to understand the process as one of grieving. We were grieving losses of childhood, needs left unfulfilled, grieving over memories of pain inflicted then buried, not dead. For some of us, memories were so buried and denial so strong that there was almost an atmosphere of, "what am I doing here?" It took time for some of the women to admit that their parents had a drinking problem or had caused them any pain. Most of us had never done much reflecting on our childhood; it had just been "that way" and for us "that way" had been "normal."

As I began the serious work of recovery, the Lord first took me through the painful process of looking closely at my relationship with my father. The dreams I had been struggling through so many nights had prepared me to reconsider my life-long perceptions of my father. Now I began to wonder if those pictures were somehow skewed. My father was wonderful, strong, happy, fun. Or was he?

February 2, 1988

It has suddenly dawned on me that as a little girl on through the teen years, I was never sure if my father loved me. The realization made me cry—I didn't feel loved. He would brag about my accomplishments, but usually he was drunk at the time. He would never play with me, he didn't talk to me except to joke around, he never disciplined me or entered into my life, and he never once said that he loved me. It was my <u>mother</u> who would tell me that he loved me and always just after he did something awful or scary. It was reassurance and I tried to believe her, but the message was confusing.

February 17, 1988

While driving in the car today, I heard a song on the radio that caused such pain and anger. The lyrics are about a little boy who is afraid of being alone and needs help and to each of the child's needs, the Daddy replies, "That's my job- be there for you and make you feel safe." As a child, somehow it didn't occur to me that caring for me in that way had been his job. In fact, it has only been as I watched Michael father our children that I have come to see what was missing for me. It had been his job and he didn't do it, and all the while I was growing up, I was trying to do it for him, making up for his lacking. I see such shame and guilt in me; he didn't want to be my Daddy is how it felt. How many times did I listen to him yelling about how tied down he was by his family, how different his life would have been without us? So I'm left feeling unworthy and unlovable. I'm left a pain, a pebble in his shoe. I think all these years, I have seen myself as failing my parents. But if anyone was failing in that situation, it was certainly them.

For a period of time, old memories washed over me in relentless succession. I remembered the nights he would be delivered to our door by a policeman because he had been too drunk to drive home from the bar. I could see again, his form stretched on the living room floor, passed out and snoring and myself stepping carefully over him to the front door to let in my date. I recalled and felt again the anguish and terror of one night on our boat, the rain pelting my face and the wind tossing us, rolling us side to side and my father screaming that we would all be smashed on the rocks and killed. I remembered the night he held my mother around the neck and while laughing crazily he plunged a hunting knife again and again into the wall behind her, just inches from her throat. When I ran screaming, it was my mother who came to me, and her words, "Everything's fine— he loves us" brought no reassurance but I froze and pretended everything was fine. We never talked about it again.

February 15, 1988

Last night I woke in the middle of the night and I was thinking about my father. I was remembering when he died and how <u>*numb*</u> *I had been. As I remembered, I thought through each event and intellectually considered each of the feelings I must have been suppressing. It was as though I was holding it away from myself, testing the depth of pain. I know I felt so clearly that there was no one to take care of me, so I couldn't let go and fall apart. The intensity of my real feelings had been so great yet I never consciously realized what those feelings were. Fear—I well remember walking alone in the dark to the boat mooring that night, shining the flashlight in front of me to keep from stumbling on the roots and weedy ground. I was calling "Daddy...?" piercing the dark silence with hope. But the mooring was empty and he was gone. He had left that morning to change the oil in the engine and he was long overdue. I went to bed that night totally numb, never considering what this might mean. Even the next morning when my mother told me that the Coast Guard had found the boat washed ashore and no one on board, still I was frozen. Even when, three days later, his body was found, there was no reaction, I shed no tears. I remember crying only once, after the funeral. I opened up to no one and I told everyone I was fine. Inside, though, I was filled with overwhelming fear and such a mighty rage. I watched my mother dissolve before my eyes as she retreated more and more into herself. She became more irrational and vague. She was trying to cope and heavily medicated. One day while driving me home from school, she rode up over the curb without ever realizing she had left the road. On the one occasion I told her I was afraid and sad, and she lashed out at me, declaring I had only lost a father and had no idea what it meant to lose a husband. This reinforced my feeling of aloneness and abandonment.*

A friend of the family came for an extended stay, trying, I think, to keep my mother glued together. Her attitude toward me was harsh; I was told in no uncertain terms to leave my mother alone. But that left me entirely on the outside. No one to talk to and always smiling, pretending I was fine.

Chapter 14

There is really no way to describe the pain of remembering these old pictures. The frozenness that had protected me as a child was now gone and I was thawing to the anguish. Most of the time I clung to the knowledge that God was taking me through this for my good and my healing. Sometimes, though, it all would seem too much.

February 24, 1988

Yesterday I was angry all day for having to go through all this pain and readjustment. I've never liked the <u>process</u> aspect of life; I always wanted the finished product, all tidy, perfect, organized and safe. I wanted to arrive at happiness and simply stay there. This ebb and flow stuff is the reality I've been denying and fighting for years.

Last night's dream took me to a world undergoing radical changes. I was told by someone that when I woke, my bed would be 100 feet down in a hole. In my dream I woke and sure enough, there I was, 100 feet down in a hole. I crawled up the side of the hole and saw the "enemy" with huge mallets, waiting to squash me flat if I climbed over the side of the hole. I fell back in the hole and felt momentarily trapped, when suddenly Scripture about the Lord's protection and love came flowing from my mouth. So, clinging to that, I climbed out again and the "mallet men" were gone. When I really did wake up, I was sure the dream was one of trust and I felt called back into God's loving arms.

I've been studying Romans for months now, but this morning I hit the old familiar chapter 8 and read with new eyes. I think I saw a new

depth of grace today. If I <u>have</u> the Spirit, which I <u>do</u>, then I will live by
the spirit and I am <u>being</u> conformed <u>by</u> the Spirit. It doesn't say "<u>Have</u>
the Spirit you rotten girl and <u>be</u> transformed, or else!" That had been
the threat of this passage to me in the past. There is no condemnation
and He is at work. That gives me such freedom and renews my joy.
Sigh...such an old, simple concept and yet how we do fight it!

March 20, 1988

I've got such a heavy heart. I don't understand why I'm hurting so
much. It comes in waves and is as intense as last fall. But I've learned
so much and come so far??!

I'm grappling with the issue of why I feel so afraid and <u>so</u> respon-
sible for everything and everyone. My chest is tight and my nerves feel
ragged. I feel as though I could cry and cry and never stop again. It's as
though I thought I had seen the bottom of the well of pain, but now I see
that it was only a <u>false</u> bottom.

For years, my dreams were loaded with sewage images. Everything from huge holes in the ground to domestic toilets, all gushing filthy, smelly ooze. The stench was real and the noise that accompanied the pictures was audible. Finally it dawned on me that these dreams were a symbol for me

March 22, 1988

I'm so full of anger—I really see it now. <u>I'm</u> the overflowing toilet; all
that dreadful sewage flowing, slapping onto the floor is my anger. When I
feel the anger, I stop being afraid. It seems like old, ancient buried anger
that has found its way to the surface.

The experience of thawing out feelings is unlike anything else. There is nothing predict-able about it and the depth of these new emotions presents a challenge. To have lived life in a frozen, guarded state and now to be cast into a world blazing with blinding color is exhausting and strange work. It is a bit like growing a third arm; clumsy and foreign.

Anger, for me, was the most forbidden of all emotions with fear a close second. The anxiety and terror leaked out first. Then great beds of the lava of anger began to burn through my defenses. For a long period of time the waves of anger flowed. When I was certain there could be no more another would wash over me. Layers and layers of strange feelings, often un-name-able feelings, insisted on being addressed.

I had grown up like so many others, learning that feelings were dangerous. Being told either directly or indirectly that, "You shouldn't feel that way", meant deciding what feelings were appropriate and allowable and the exercise became second nature. Because all the wide range of feelings comes naturally and continually to us human beings, there had to be constant stifling and denying of feelings that were happening. It was safer to become numb than to risk a "wrong" feeling leaking out from within.

Feelings were either right or they were wrong and that was determined by my parents. My job was to make very sure I didn't upset them by feeling something that was wrong. How much safer it seemed to simply turn off feelings than to take the awful risk of getting it wrong. I remember thinking of myself as even keeled, steady, gliding through life without the precarious ups and downs of strong emotion. To my way of thinking, that was the successful, mature way to live. I had no idea at the time how much of life I was missing by this very defense mechanism I had learned in order to cope. My days had been lived in the safety zone of grey so I didn't know the spectrum of color that is life.

Somewhere in my recovery process I learned to question these long-held beliefs about feelings. What a revolutionary concept was the notion that feelings are neither right nor wrong. They are, instead, indicators of what is going on inside of us. Without those "signals" on the dashboard of our life, we have little idea who we are and what we are thinking. The challenge was to let go of the little girl belief and accept and live the truth.

The fear that if I feel whatever I am feeling, including the punishable feelings of fear or anger, I'll meet some terrible consequence and be "bad" is a mighty and sticky fear. Changing my belief system as an adult was no easy task. The roots of those beliefs run to my core. It is not surprising that there is a lot of work involved in letting go of the old lies and grasping onto the truth. As a believer in God and His Son Jesus, I had a "leg up" in this important work. I knew that the truth comes from God and the world is full of lies and deceit. From the moment we turn to the Lord and surrender ourselves to Him, we are in the process of discarding the world's lies and grasping God's truth. So this work of understanding and turning toward the truth about our feelings is more of the same. Because we belong to God, we have His Spirit to guide and empower us in the journey and that is our hope in our recovery.

It is when we are honest and "thawed out" about our feelings that we are able to address our thinking. This is the reverse of how we learned to function in the feeling arena early in life. We would think, or decide, what we should feel, or not feel, and by doing so, force ourselves to be or appear to be the approvable person. "I am not afraid so I am calm and not threatened by what is happening. I am not angry and so I am happy."

Instead of this backwards way of feeling and thinking, that is, deciding how we should feel instead of being honest about how we really *are* feeling, if we would feel what we are feeling honestly and currently, we would know where our heart is and how the Lord might want to correct and nudge us. It is in knowing our real feelings that we begin to know ourselves. "I am really angry. Why am I so angry? What am I thinking that is making me feel so angry? Am I thinking this because I am believing the truth or because I am believing a lie?" First the feelings that demonstrate what we believe and who we are, and then the work of addressing what is revealed.

One of the reasons this work of feeling what we are really feeling and being who we really are is so painfully and fearfully difficult is that we experience so much shame in our very core over who we are. We believe in our heart of hearts that we are unacceptable and discard-able. Perhaps unwanted and certainly disappointing. We spent our childhood never measuring up in some way or in every way. We adopt the lifelong struggle of monitoring every feeling and every indication of failure on our part in order to be perfect and perfectly acceptable. Feelings are a wild thing; unruly, often surprising and full of power. If we let them out, surely they will betray us and we will be found out to be the broken down person we know ourselves to really be. Facing that truth about our brokenness and that fear of being nothing is the door to the freedom of knowing Christ and His redemption.

John 3:16 tells us God gave His Son for us so that if we believe and surrender to Him, we have life and are not condemned. I John 3:1 resonates with the love God has lavished on us, making us his children. A perfect Father, with a perfect love, gives us a new beginning and a new chance at childhood. In Hebrews 13:5-6 we read His declaration that "Never will I leave you; never will I forsake you. The Lord is my helper; I will not be afraid. What can man do to me?" That describes a place of safety and certainty we probably never knew at home. His blood sacrifice makes us clean and completely acceptable, dearly loved by our Father, and washes away the shame we have carried all our lives.

Realizing we no longer are sentenced to a life of covering up our imperfections and that we are fully known by a loving Father who recognizes our brokenness *and has done something about it*, brings unimaginable freedom. It is like letting go of a concrete chest of shame and growing wings; free from covering up and free to face God, other people and ourselves. Instead of living a self-focused life constricted by the constant need to deny and "image manage", we begin to let go enough to live a creative life of service to Him and others.

Chapter 15

Coming to terms with memories of my father proved easier for me than those of my mother. My relationship with my mother was complicated by a strange "fusing" that had taken place between us. Somehow the boundaries of our identities became confused and I had melded into her being, losing my own personhood. Because my father was unable to be the husband she needed, she placed me in that role. I was her closest friend, her counselor, her constant companion in a way that stunted my growth and isolated me from other people. Even more costly, though was the effect on my identity. My feelings, my thoughts and reactions needed always to be carefully screened if I was to avoid her anger or disappointment and threaten my own security. Somewhere along the way, I lost my ability to think for myself.

While I listened to my friends in the ACOA group talk about their current struggles in relating to their parents, I puzzled over my own difficulties talking about my mother and father. These women struggled with *living* parents; mine were long dead. How strange that in reality they didn't feel dead at all! In some peculiar ritual of habit, I had lived for them all these years, still playing the part of the "good girl" (meaning the compliant, trouble-free girl) and squelching full expression of myself. Still a little girl, I had missed the pulling-away-to-independence stage so natural and important to the teenage years.

Now I found myself a thirty-six year old teenager, ready at last to test her limits and her wings. I began slowly to separate myself from my mother, silencing the old voices in my head and making choices that expressed the personhood I found emerging. I began to be less afraid to speak my own opinion, to show my real feelings. The freedom I began to experience was heady !

March 23, 1988

I feel myself again and again making choices and I feel like a giddy college gal who just moved out and for the first time is experiencing independence!

Along with the euphoria of breaking away, though, came the torrents of confusion and guilt. The long- buried anger that I was experiencing was new to me and frightening. To allow myself to see and feel the anger toward my mother was a move toward independence, and for me, the unknown. It seemed so irrational to fear losing her when she was dead; it seemed irrational to be angry at all because I knew she had loved me, she had tried. Irrational or not, though, the hurt and the anger were still with me.

March 28, 1988

Yesterday I wrote a letter to my mother and released so much anger. I sobbed my way through it and when I reread it I was surprised at some of what I had written. It was very hard to start writing; loyalty to her and to the lie of our idyllic life was going strong. This allegiance makes it so hard to feel and express the anger I feel toward her. I had always felt like her protector and sensed her fragility. I see how hard it was to communicate my true feelings to my dead *mother made me realize how I held onto her all these years. I haven't, until now,* wanted *to be free.*

"Mama,

If you were truly here, I doubt that I could say these things to you. Even knowing that you will not see them, I am afraid to tell you how angry I am with you. You always seemed so fragile, and I wanted to protect you. But I wanted <u>you</u> *to take care of me! I wanted you to make me feel secure and safe; I wanted to know that you would never leave me again.*

I think I was so angry, hurt and confused when you were drinking—I don't remember much, but I do remember feeling alone. I remember not understanding how you could leave me alone when I was such a little girl. I wanted my mommy so badly and there was no comfort for me.

All the while growing up I felt trapped in some kind of track. I had to behave so carefully or you would get so angry at me. I grew up desperately afraid of anger; anger meant sudden violence and sure chaos; anger meant someone was leaving. I never told you how angry and afraid I was. I never crossed you willfully. I was so careful, careful, careful. I never tried, I never reached, I never flew!

When you died, I was so angry, Angry, ANGRY! You told me not to come see you that day. You went to the hospital that night and you didn't call me. You died. You left me again! I took care of you all those years and you left me."

The letter sounds like the ranting of a little girl and I suppose that's actually what it is. I felt a release in owning up to those traitorous feelings and with tiny scissors I began to cut away the cords that bound me to her.

Getting in touch with the anger was the first crucial step I took toward forgiveness and peace. My biggest fear as I uncovered the layers and layers of pain was that I would spend the rest of my life covered in the sticky debris. Instead, I discovered the joy of letting it go. As long as the anger stayed buried it festered and smoldered, even though invisible to me all those years.

Chapter 16

At first the entire concept of forgiving escaped me. How could I forgive my parents if they didn't intend to hurt me? The need to forgive implied that they had done something wrong and from the beginning my sense of loyalty would not allow any wrong-doing on their part. As I began to see how frightened and hurt I had been as a little girl, I began to feel pain for that child and to embrace her with empathy. In doing that, I saw that though my parents had never intended to hurt me, and had in fact loved me in the only way they were able, still I had suffered great pain. They hadn't meant to hurt me, but they had and I was justifiably angry.

I discovered that while anger had been an elusive concept for me, forgiveness was an entirely mysterious act. Somehow in my mind, forgiving someone had gotten tangled up with pretending that I wasn't angry or hurt; too much lava of emotion had flowed to continue that illusion! I knew also that I didn't want to become sucked back into pretending that all was well and my pain didn't matter because that felt like saying I don't matter. How could I forgive my mother and father if that required stuffing emotion or resigning my newly forming personhood? Copping out was no longer an option for me. I *had* to find out how to forgive in a healthy manner.

Complicating the scenario was the knowledge that, though my parents had indeed failed to be perfect parents or even the parents I needed them to be-I still loved them. I didn't like the way they acted, the things they did, and I mourned the loss of the family I wished we could have been, but I loved them. Along with all the painful memories, I had also stowed away precious and positive remembrances between folds of gossamer to protect the recollections I treasured. There was my father's evident pride when I practiced my clarinet and the way he called it my "licorice stick" and put me in a class with Benny Goodman. The night I found my beloved parakeet cold and stiff on the floor of his cage, Daddy didn't say much, but he listened to me cry and helped me bury him in a humble shoe box.

My mother had taken more than I had to give as a little girl, but she let me curl in her lap one day in junior high and cry over my first romantic jilting. She met me all those days for lunch when I couldn't face the cafeteria in second grade and she told me she loved me many times.

Learning to forgive meant letting go of the warped notion that, just because they had been my parents and I loved them, I couldn't be hurt by or angry with them. What I found was that the art of forgiving is a spiritual exercise. The depth of letting go and healing that forgiveness requires, is outside the puny realm of human ability. I had to ask God to give me the ability to forgive and let go. I needed to look at each memory as the Lord called them back to me, experience the accompanying pain, and for every one be able to say, "You hurt me." I was so afraid, lost, confused, and alone. Though I understand that you were hurting too, you sinned against me and that hurt and it made me angry. Through the power of God and **His** forgiveness of **me, I** forgive **you**. I no longer hold what you did against you." This was work; it required time. I had to fully feel the pain and the anger, and forgive, before I was ready to move on.

This letting go was a process; the process was different for each woman in my ACOA group. While some seemed to let go and forgive all at once, I found that I needed to forgive in layers as the Lord took me deeper into the pain. As long as the memories flowed, I was accosted with new hurt and anger so I was moving in a swirling sea of remembering and forgiving.

As time passed, the memories slowed and stopped and I sensed that the bulk of the work of forgiving my parents had been done. Slowly the realization that something miraculous had taken place began to settle into my consciousness; the parents that had pulled and pushed at me, demanded from me, hurt and frightened me even twenty years after their death, were finally buried. To be angry and hurt means to hang on and never to be free from the pain. To forgive means that God can bring healing. I was free.

It was startling to realize that the anger I hoarded, thinking it would protect me from hurtful parents, instead tied me to the very hurt I wanted to escape. It was only through forgiving that I became unstuck from the trauma and my parents stopped controlling my emotions and my life. I found the freedom I longed for in letting go.

Chapter 17

At first I thought that finishing the work of forgiveness meant being *finished*—complete, no pain, done and over! Instead, sometimes flashbacks were triggered by everyday events and hurt or anger would rear up. I knew that Satan wanted me to take the anger back and hang onto the pain because he knows that very pain is my destruction. When those incited hurts returned, I again had to let go of what I held against my parents in order to be free. I wanted to be able to forgive the way the Lord forgives me, holding nothing against me while giving me a clean slate and new beginnings. There was much prayer work involved in the process and again I found the Lord to be faithful. The healing that sprang from this step of forgiveness was dramatic.

April 4, 1988

It was a full and really good long weekend. I continue to feel as though I have passed through a certain depth of mourning and come out the other side.

Friday night I dreamed another one worth remembering. I went to some sort of farm, taking along an ax because I knew that I had some important chopping to do. The "authorities" there were chasing me; my heart was pumping as I determined my way forward, but I wasn't really afraid. I think I was off to sever my fusing ties to my parents and to declare my independence.

Yesterday afternoon as I sat with the Lord, I was thinking about the difference between isolation and loneliness. All my life I have called the feeling loneliness, but really I was feeling isolated; alone, cut off, different, locked away. I was abandoned, unlovable. After unlocking those secret doors and sharing the pain through counseling and in group, and getting to know this person inside, the isolation is gone for the first time in my life. Even in my intimacy with Michael, part of me was locked away and isolated. Now I can feel lonely, but lonely can be remedied—loneliness is self-imposed; isolation is a prison.

Forgiving my parents was a major key to healing for me but it wasn't the only truth that was setting me free. I was sensitized to my feelings now and that meant many uncomfortable moments, encumbered with an anguish that bade me escape. Even though I was compulsively running less, still I felt an anxious, emotional kind of bolting that left me exhausted and tense.

April 19, 1988

Another very restless night's sleep. I wake in the middle of the night almost every night now, feeling tense and "hyper". My heart is racing, my stomach is churning and I feel as though I'm running and I can't stop. It takes a while to fall asleep and in the morning I'm exhausted! My dreams haven't been clear, but they seem filled with ACOA struggles. I feel like I can't <u>rest</u> anymore. It's as though there is a monster inside of me, driving me, or a dragon pursuing me. I want to shoot it with a tranquilizer gun and make it be still and rest, but it will not.

I guess what I'm feeling is very divided. When I sleep, I come face to face with this other part of me that's running so scared. The restless pull is there during the day too and I've given in to it some in the name of spring cleaning. But even when I sit to read or pray, the churning tight chest and nervous feelings keep me from relaxing. I feel like an animal that's been cornered.

It was obvious that, though I was more in touch with my feelings and my pain in particular, I still didn't know what to do with them. My way of coping had always been two-fold; run from the feelings by denial or achievement, or fix the situation or the feeling. This method of dealing with pain had made me a mover with a mission, but when the circumstances couldn't be fixed or I was too tired to run anymore, I was in deep trouble.

This is exactly what had happened in my breakdown. I had denied and stuffed since childhood, then adding the insecurity and pain of our move to New Jersey to the submerged pile of trauma, I had run and run until my body had finally cried out "Enough!". Because I knew no other method of coping, my counselor's words directing me to allow myself to "feel the feeling" instead of running from the pain never quite got past my head. I heard the words; I thought I understood, but still when I felt pain, the old habits kicked in and I'd be running or fixing. Then one day in prayer, the Lord pulled back the veil and there was a sunrise of truth that brought a new level of peace.

April 20, 1988

I think I finally heard what has been said to me over and over; what I have read and even said to myself, but somehow didn't quite see—I have to feel the feelings! So this is new??!! It's as though a layer has been penetrated and I finally understand that these painful, uncomfortable, intrusive feelings are a part of the process of recovery…are a part of life…and I've at last acquiesced to feel it, not fix it. I've always presumed that the uncomfortable feelings got in the way of living, now I think I understand that they are living. It's an enigma to me how I can hear words over and over and be dense to them.

The feelings themselves were no longer a threat to me. Before when I felt strong emotional discomfort, I was driven to escape, much like an alcoholic escapes pain by retreating into an alcoholic blur. I medicated myself with denial or compulsive activity and achievement because staying in the feeling wasn't an option. Now I began to practice feeling the feeling, sitting in it and finding it didn't swallow me up or kill me. I could admit it, talk about it, perhaps make creative changes or even, with God's help, accept it.

This was a tremendous change for me! To experience the feeling instead of running from it was not the same as wallowing in the emotion. In fact, feelings made me so uncomfortable that avoiding them was more my style. I wasn't now stagnating in the emotion; I was merely allowing myself to *feel* pain without running.

Later I would learn that my feelings are not my enemies but actually my friend. Without my feelings, I would never know myself and what I believe. Those feelings I had fought against and numbed out of awareness were the indicator lights on my dashboard. They told me what I believe and what kind of person I am. An event occurs, my mind processes the event through my "filter" that is made up of what I believe to be true, and my feelings come as a reaction to that belief system. Instead of attacking the feeling with the machete of denial, what I needed to do was embrace the feeling, *feel the feeling,* and thereby become aware of what I believe about the event. Then I know myself better. If the feeling reveals that I am believing something that isn't true, I can look at that erroneous belief, confess is it is sin, and turn to the truth. Feelings give me the opportunity to grow and change my life. It was slow for me but eventually I could see that my feelings are the color in my life, the spice, the scent that gives me my own unique fragrance. My feelings expressed my personhood.

Chapter 18

One of the painful feelings that continued to rear its unwanted head was the suspicion that I was unlovable and unwanted. I had spent so much time and effort in my life covering up this sense of being disposable that I was unaware of the ache it caused. To cope, I had striven and struggled to make myself indispensable to those around me; to somehow make a place for a person who didn't really belong. The concept of personhood was very foreign to me. I had spent my life bending to other people's needs and beliefs. Not only did I not have my own feelings but I had no sense of being an individual. Alone, I was worthless.

April 1, 1988

I've mused a lot about the concept of feeling basically unlovable—the Lord has been showing me how deep that misgiving goes, and how it affects my life. My gut is so sure I'm unacceptable…

I didn't see this self-loathing for quite awhile. The feelings had been a submerged part of me all my life. I was accustomed to them. They were unexplored and had no name or source. In fact, I well remember leafing through a recommended ACOA textbook and spotting a chapter titled "Shame". I can still feel the strong relief I felt then, "knowing" that at least *that* was one problem I *didn't* have to confront! Of course the Lord knew better and was already in the process of gently reaching into the soft rotting parts of my heart, preparing to expose that decayed mass to the fresh air.

One of the reasons my shame was hard to see was that it had very deep roots entombed in a childhood of denied and skewed memories. As long as I saw my parents as model people that were always there for me and my re-united family as the "second-chance family" that made it work, then there was no way for me to grasp the pain and shame I was really feeling in their neglect and my separation from them.

Slowly, as the memories unfolded before me and God gave me new adult eyes to perceive my childhood, the layers of shame were exposed also. I began to understand that when my parents were drinking or struggling with their own pain and unavailable to me, I believed in my childish heart that it was my fault. When I was surrendered to my grandparents, there was no way for me to comprehend why I was being turned away. I can remember even now the feeling of anguish and rejection those early years at my grandparents' home, face down in my pillow asking why everyone else had a mommy and daddy except me. When my father wasn't emotionally present for me or when my mother was upset, it was my fault, shame on ME. Even later in my teens, when I could see that my father or something else quite tangible was causing my mother's pain or anger, still somehow *I* felt the compulsion to make her happy, to make everything all right. So if I failed to "fix it", then that was to my shame too. And because there was so much pain, so many things to fix so often, my shame grew to enormous proportions.

Looking back, I can see how the Lord was dealing with this "unloveableness" when He first called me to Himself as a teenager. That encounter was made dramatic for me in the new-found knowledge that I was *not* unlovable after all. Jesus Christ, the Son of God, knew me and loved me. He was calling me to belong to Him and for a sixteen year old who had never felt the joy and safety of belonging to anyone, or anywhere, this was good news indeed. How easy it is for me now to look back and see the Lord wooing me and the eagerness with which I followed Him. I needed His love so desperately and I continue to depend upon that safe place of being cared for and loved.

I found my growing connection with Christ to be like any other beginning relationship. The more time I spent with Him, reading the Bible and talking with Him in prayer, the better I knew Him. My flourishing relationship with the Lord touched my feelings of shame on two levels. If Christ could die for me personally, then that was an overwhelming declaration not only of love, but He was proclaiming and making me a non-dispensable person. He wasn't throwing me out or giving me away. He was giving Himself up in order to *keep me*. His death on that cross was perfect proof that I was loved and I had a place to belong.

The second level of shame the Lord dealt with was one of real shame. The first was simply perceived shame; I had seen myself as unlovable and faulty, someone to be rejected because I had felt rejected as a child. But as I began to know Christ better, I began to see that there was a *real* shame problem as well. How far short I fell of the perfect pot I was to be in the hands of my potter, God. I didn't obey Him or love Him as I wanted or as He deserved and the word "sin" became a reality for me. Some of my shame was very well deserved! God's sacrifice of His Son meant that God no longer held that sin against me. In fact, Scripture told me that He no longer even *saw* that sin. For me, it was a wonderful one-two punch; the real shame I felt of being so much less than the person I was created to be was covered over by Christ's blood and His own perfection. The nagging voice in my heart telling me I was unwanted and unlovable was silenced by His death because now I knew there was something in me worth redeeming.

So in my early walk with the Lord, my feelings of inadequacy and shame were addressed and I never guessed there were deeper layers for the Lord to pull out and heal. I needed God to lovingly swipe the scales of denial about my childhood from my eyes before the core of my shame could be exposed. As a sixteen year old I only sensed my feelings of fear and isolation. Now as a grown woman with more realistic sight, I could more fully appreciate the enormity of God's call to me. His love bade me come to Him; His grace made that possible.

Old habits die hard, though, and I think old ways of thinking die even harder! The truth about who I am in Christ is real and a part of my mind now, yet I still react as though I'm unacceptable and unredeemed. I can see that this will be a life-long struggle of *believing* what Christ says about me above the old voices in my head and my deepest fears. It is a battle of surrendering my old way of thinking to Him. The Bible calls it putting off the old and putting on the new mind of Christ. Along the way, there are little skirmishes and victories but the conflict wages on. The ammunition continues to be God's word loaded into my head, reprogramming my thinking by the power of the Holy Spirit so that I may more fully know how loved and accepted I am in Christ. What incredible freedom to be found under the wings of my Savior! Released from the bondage of shame and performance, I'm free to look into Christ's eyes. Unfettered, unshackled feet can follow the Master with enthusiasm and true devotion in a way that no one carrying a heavy sack filled with self- embarrassment and loathing ever could.

Chapter 19

The spring bursting forth around me was a graphic image of the growth that was taking place within. While the world changed clothes from the drab barrenness of winter to the gay finery of spring, my gray heart was taking on the colors of health. A monumental milestone was my new grasp on the process aspect of life. Being in perpetual flux had caused me so much insecurity that the idea of being always in process was horrifying. My goal had been to get it done, get it over with and get past it! I had approached my breakdown and recovery in this way and now I was realizing my whole life had been the struggle to "complete". If I am indeed at peace with God the way I am, then suddenly there is joy in the *process* of life. There is room to grow, to be refined and refining. There is room to be on God's great drawing board. There is room to be imperfect, to be wrong. One day in April it dawned on me that there had been a subtle but oh so important change in my thinking:

April 18, 1988

Only a work of His spirit will heal that part of me and he is obviously well into the process. Hey! Process! I'm actually beginning to like that dumb word!

That spring there were critical changes in my perception of my childhood trauma too. These changes seemed to release some sort of block within me as though I had been struggling to withhold this information from myself. What followed was a new sense of peace. I felt as though I had given my subconscious the final permission to let go of its secrets and rest.

April 20, 1988

The ideas about the changes in my perception of my origin of pain came to a head this morning talking to Susanne. Before my breakdown, I saw my abandonment time as the most painful. Leaving my parents for almost five years seemed the greatest source of grief. Then, at the beginning of the destruction of my denial system, I experienced great pain and anger toward my parents for leaving me. From there I came to terms with my father's alcoholism and how that had hurt me. Slowly I realized my hurt and disappointment toward my mother, releasing hidden anger.

A three-part picture began to develop: 1) my mother's drinking before our family broke up, 2) time at my grandparents' house, and 3) our reunited family, when my father's drinking became a problem. As I perceived the trauma in three parts instead of simply focusing on my abandonment to my grandparents' home, I could look anew at the overall episode which represented the source of my past pain. As a result, I began to grieve for my grandparents and a refocused picture of my days spent with them emerged.

Though my mind has erased much of the early transition, the memories begin again as a happy six year old. What shocked me next was the realization that it was the reunion of my nuclear family when I was eight, jarring me from the relatively secure nest of Grandma and Grandpa which was perhaps the greatest source of pain during the entire period. The "second chance" with Mama and Daddy that I had grown up deeming a source of joy had actually been a "second hell." It was seeing the juxtaposition of a relatively secure and happy time at my grandparents' with the ugliness and disappointment of family life after age eight that knocked down the last few cards of fantasy still balancing precariously in my deck of denial.

The Lord took all those months to pull memories from me with flash- backs and amazing dreams and now He was helping me sort through the components of my life, refiling, and preparing to finally close the cabinet drawer. As a little girl I had filed "abandonment" under pain and "reunited family" under joy. God emptied the file cabinet, throwing all those perceptions into the wind of His spirit, and now that it was time to refile, the placement was reversed. To me, this is an incredible change. I have broken through much denial and unhealthy loyalty.

April 25, 1988

I've been much more relaxed lately and sleeping great with no night-mares for a week or so. In fact, I'm having ordinary, mundane dreams reminiscent of the way I used to dream.

Since the realization that my most painful experience in growing up was when my family reunited, I have felt more peaceful. The night-mares and overflowing toilets have stopped. I can't help but feel that I have come over some hump; around some bend in the road; feel...more emptied of pain than I have in all these months.

The fruit of healing that spring was evident from my journal entries. Each day a new discovery unfolded and feelings became a normal part of reacting to life. Disappointment and confusion popped up at regular intervals but there was a new tolerance to pain and process.

April 28, 1988

Yesterday was a day to marvel at growth. It was a busy day attending to household tasks, errands, groceries, and by afternoon I was cooking dinner for a friend in need and encouraging another on the telephone. I watched myself in awe—only months ago I couldn't cook my own family's dinner!

I think that I'm starting to really let go of a lot of the guilt I've carried. I don't find it coming up in the every- day situations so I think God has been dealing with the deeper level of leftover childhood shame of which I grew up so unaware. I feel less encumbered by the "shoulds."

(Not the good "should" which come from the spirit and Word of God, but the wrong "should" which comes from the Accuser.) The Spirit makes me aware of how He is using me to touch lives and I'm finding more of a ministry in prayer than ever before. I'm still surprised to realize over and over again that other people value me; that I have a place in this world and God wants to use me in His Plan. Somehow there's a difference between struggling to make myself indispensable and being valued for myself. I guess I'm enjoying "being!"

I was rereading the entries in this journal made just a month ago and I'm astounded at the changes! There is in me a newly developing healthy disentanglement from others—not detached, but separate, I guess. I feel boundaries developing. I can see others grieve or have stress and sympathize while NOT carry the responsibility. I think I'm beginning to trust God in a new way. I know I'm allowing the Lord to take care of me; I've come a long way from pulling Christ in my heavy cart! I'm trusting Him to care for others too; to be used in service to Him, but with the responsibility on His shoulders not mine. He is in control and I am His vessel.

May 2, 1988

I continue on, sleeping like a rock every night—no nightmares and no remembered dreams. Sometimes when I think ahead, I get very nervous, but mostly I seem not to be so future focused. It is as though I have gotten into the habit of believing that each day is sufficient unto itself—surely its troubles are! There's a new feeling of being more alive each moment of today, becoming more aware of my emotions as they happen and giving myself room to stop and feel instead of racing ahead to accomplish, to finish. This somehow makes me more flexible and able to ride the waves the Lord sends my way.

May 4, 1988

Today I turn 36—can't decide whether that's old or young. Maybe it's neither; another gray area! I'm learning not to be quite so black and white, quite so definite and extreme.

Michael and I went out to dinner last night to celebrate my birthday because today we have lacrosse practice that he coaches, in addition to Kate's softball game and Young Life. We spent the whole time at dinner talking about balancing the pastorate with the family, our ever-present struggle. The discussion was painful for me, but helpful and invigorating for Michael. He feels that his picture of a good husband and father are in contradiction with his concept of the ideal pastor. Hence, we have a no-win situation.

Our conversation really tied into my fear of the dragon—that beast of duty and burden who takes away my choices and tells me what I must do, that what I do is never enough, and that my heart's desires don't matter. This dragon has always been hard to put into words, yet he is so very real.

By bedtime I was so full of terror that I was in tears. The healing and health I have found are like tissue paper butterfly wings; so fragile. It seems that just when I think I have arrived at wholeness, I fall over some kind of cliff and get pulled back into the hard place. My habit is always to think of healing as a finished product, dusting off my hands and declaring, "There! I'm done." But that is just not so. Even so, I've found this quiet peace—the very edges of it, but the promise of a firm grip to come. This peace is a quietness and contentedness that drifts over me, and is not based on circumstances, but built on peace with myself and the world as it really is, the illusions gone. It is all about how I think about myself and the world and not determined by what is coming at me from the outside. I have such a sense of expressing myself as God created me to be that is new. Before, I buried myself in duties and performance and the future. There's joy in caring for my family, relating to my God and reaching out to others in such a natural, spiritual way. I feel excitement—as though I woke up from a 35 year long sleep to discover I'm an interesting person with God-given depths to express. God is calling me to listen; there is much work to do in the Kingdom and I must not become confused about my place. He appoints my gifts and burdens and sends me out to express His work and nature in the unique way He designed for me. Because of that divine calling and equipping, I'm learning that I can serve Him in health and joy instead of running for my life as the dragon breathes fire at my heels.

Even as my Savior heals me from within, He is battling the dragon with piercing swords. May that dragon be vanquished forever!

May 6, 1988

I'm looking out the window at my cherry tree blooming with delicate pink petals bursting from their buds. Last fall when I was so broken and immersed in pain, that cherry tree was my symbol of hope. "When my cherry tree blooms," I wrote then, "I'll be better!"

And, praise be to my God, I am!

EPILOGUE

If I were to end the story here, I would be guilty of leaving the impression that there <u>is</u> an end to this journey. How easy to wrap all the pain up in a neat phrase, "Now I'm better!" The most important lesson God has been teaching me, though, is that life isn't like that. My life is not a boxwood garden, precision rows, a neat beginning, a simple ending. Instead, my life is a free-floating mobile with all the components moving, swaying, surprising me with each turn. Though I do not control those dynamic parts, my God holds the mobile tightly in His Hand and it is the wind of His Spirit that directs the components of my life.

One of the ways God directed me came as a <u>real</u> surprise. Fifteen years after my breakdown and the start of my recovery work, I set out to develop a Bible Study for women like me, who had grown up in homes that didn't feel safe. It was going to be just a ten week study to pass on some of what God had been teaching me about my own brokenness and pain. The lonely, lost and wrenching horror of barely surviving those childhood traumas was not something I was going to forget. And the intense pain that brought me to my physical and emotional breakdown was raw enough to be etched in my heart forever. I will never forget what it is like to be at that place. Because of that, the freedom of facing the lies and the truths, and then beginning to move on, putting my childhood behind me at last, was something too big, too amazing, to keep to myself. I was bursting to share it with others like me.

The short ten week study grew into a program of not only a year long study but support groups as well. <u>All of this</u> has surprised me. Every year I watch more and more women touched by God's healing truth. Every year I am reminded that He has taken the trauma of my childhood and my own brokenness to mend other lives. What a great God He is! I say this often and it is heart-felt, "God never wastes any pain". I am grateful that He is using mine.

THE
EBENEZER
PROGRAM

THE HISTORY OF THE EBENEZER PROGRAM

The Ebenezer program didn't begin as a "program". It started simply as a ten class study addressing the affects of having grown-up in a severely dysfunctional home. Through my own healing process and experience in Christian counseling and participation in a Christian Adult Children of Alcoholics group during the 1980's, God planted a seed in my heart to reach back and offer to others what He had so mercifully provided for me. I grew up in a home with two alcoholic parents and was mostly unaware of how that had affected me until my mid-thirties when a life-time of denial and running caught up with me.

Having been a Christian since 1969 and a pastor's wife for fifteen years, I had been a retreat speaker and taught many Bible studies over the years, and so it was natural for me to begin to think in terms of putting together a class to address childhood issues. God continued to work in me for the next thirteen years (there was a lot of work to be done!) before the time was right to begin the first class in 2001.

Searching for a name for the group, I scanned through Scriptures and the word "Ebenezer" seemed to jump from the page. I Samuel 7:12 says, "Then Samuel took a stone and set it up between Mizpah and Shen. He named it Ebenezer, saying, 'Thus far has the Lord helped us.' "Rock of Help"-what better name could there be for a group of people who were once helpless children subjected to unsafe environments, neglect and abuse surviving because our God had kept us; our God who will be our Great Physician if we will yield ourselves to Him.

When I wrote the material, I fully expected these original ten classes to be the extent of the project. But our Lord is full of wonderful surprises! When the participants from the first class were nearing the final class, they asked, "SO, what's next? We're not done yet! We haven't talked about this, or this, or…" I knew they were right so I spent a snowy January writing the next ten classes which became Ebenezer II. Both Ebenezer I and II are set up as a teaching experience with some discussion.

Of course, I was certain I was done then! After the "graduates" completed Ebenezer II, they had another question for me: '"Where will we find another group setting as safe as this one has been, where we can continue in the process of healing?" Actually, what they said was, "Are you going to dump us now?"

The experience of discovering that we are not alone in our experiences and struggles with childhood trauma was too new and wonderful to end. And so Ebenezer III was born; a support group of "graduates" where we can continue to grow and practice the scriptural truths we learned in Ebenezer I and II. Each spring the new group of "graduates" (having completed both Ebenezer I and II) is enfolded into the larger group. The support group meets monthly. Each month one of the group acts as the "presenter", choosing the topic for discussion in advance of the meeting and may choose to simply throw it out to the group or bring a full-blown presentation, depending on comfort level and choice.

As Ebenezer has grown, the need for additional leaders prompted the Leader's Training class, designed to equip others to lead Ebenezer groups.

As I watch the unfolding of God's surprises with the Ebenezer program, one passage keeps coming to mind: "Now to Him who is able to do immeasurably more than all we ask or imagine, according to his power that is at work within us, to him be glory in the church and in Christ Jesus throughout all generations for ever and ever! Amen." Ephesians 3:20. I watch in awe and excitement as He continues His work. What a privilege to be a part of His Kingdom!

DOCTRINAL STATEMENT AND PHILOSOPHY OF MINISTRY FOR THE EBENEZER PROGRAM

The Ebenezer program is firmly based on the Word of God, which are the Scriptures. In the Word of God we find the Truth and it is in recognizing the Lies we have believed and replacing them with God's Truth that we are "transformed by the renewing of (our) mind" (Romans 12:1-2) and there is hope for healing from the devastating affects of having grown up in a severely dysfunctional home.

Part of the task of embracing the Truth is the exercise of facing what happened to us as children and understanding the lies we believed in order to cope and the traits we developed as part of that coping. The Ebenezer Program is designed to create a safer environment where individuals can explore the baggage we carry with others who also are burdened with the past in the Light of God's Truth.

The goal of the Ebenezer Program is to move from facing our past, to mourning and grieving the past, to re-building the foundation of our life and our identity on Christ. "No longer being taken captive through hollow and deceptive philosophy which depends on human tradition and basic principles of this world rather than on Christ" (Colossians 2:8), we seek spiritual and emotional maturity and health.

The Ebenezer Program encourages participants to pursue healing and holiness. The recovery process is different for everyone; however, the bulk of the work should eventually be put behind. Our desire should be to find our place in the Kingdom more and more as we are freed from the past so that we may serve our God more fully. Let us "press on to take hold of that for which Christ Jesus took hold of me." (Philippians 3:12)

BIBLICAL PRINCIPLES FROM THE EBENEZER PROGRAM

God's Character and My Relationship To Him

1. God is the Light of revelation and truth- Psalm 27:1; John 3:19-21; John 1:3-5; I Peter 2:9; Psalm 18:28.

2. God is our hope- II Samuel 22:5-20, 29, 30.

3. God made me, knows me, the days ordained for me are written in His book- Psalm 139.

4. I belong to God- Psalm 16.

5. God is the source for all truth- Philippians 4:8; Psalm 25:4-5; Psalm 26:2-3; 3 John 3-4; John 14:6.

Sin and Shame

6. God sees our sin- Hebrews 4:12-13; Isaiah 55:8.

7. Jesus is the answer to our sin- John 14:6; Romans 5:6-11; 7:14-8:2.

8. Grace is the answer for our real shame- Romans 8:1-4.

9. God's love and healing are the answer to the false shame we learned in our impaired families.

10. Fear of exposure, pride and the idol of self are roots of perfectionism- Jeremiah 2:13.

11. The gospel alone has the power to heal- Psalm 18:30-32, Psalm 25:1-7, Philippians 3:1-14; Romans 3:9-20.

12. The fear that drives perfectionism is not from God- Psalm 27.

13. Perfectionism is an idol- Isaiah 44:15, 17, 20, 21, 22.

God's Grace and Restoration

14. Seeking God is the attitude that Christ lives in me- Galatians 2:20.

15. God looks on the heart- Galatians 3:1-5.

16. 16: The Lord is my shepherd and in Him I lack nothing- Psalm 23.

17. God is faithful and comforts and restores us- Isaiah 49:8-26; II Corinthians 1:3-7.

18. God teaches us about grief- Psalm 88; John 11:33-36 .

Grieving Over Sin and Forgiving/Forgiveness

19. God calls us to forgive-Psalm 32:3-4; Matt 6:9-15; 18:21-35; Luke 6: 27-45, 32-38; 7:36-50; Eph 4:32-5:2.

20. God is our "Ebenezer", our Rock of Help-Psalm 30.

God's Care For Us and Our Caring For Others

21. God gives us many great things- Psalm 103.

22. God teaches us what good personal boundaries look like- Deuteronomy 5:29; Proverbs 3:12; Job 5:17; Is 55:8; Ezekiel 16:58; II Corinthians 6:11-13; Heb 12:7-11; I John 1:9; 4:1-3.

23. God shows us what real love and Godly service to others looks like- Galatians 6:7-10.

24. We are responsible to care for others when their load is too heavy for them to bear- Galatians 6:2-5.

25. The Lord uses correction and consequences in our lives and the lives of others- Proverbs 13:18-24; 15:10.

26. Fear of man is a spiritual problem- Psalm 27:1-2; Proverbs 29:25; I John 4:18.

27. We are called to a life of love and servanthood- Philippians 2:1-18.

28. We are able to serve others when God fills us with His grace and everything we need- II Corinthians 9:6-15.

29. God tells us His values- Psalm 119:20-24; Jeremiah 9:23-24.

30. We are responsible to God- Jeremiah 10:23-24.

31. We are responsible for setting limits and boundaries for ourselves- Matt 10:11-14; 18:15-17; I Corinthians 5:9-13.

32. God shows us how a healthy relationship looks- Romans 12:3-5, 9-21.

33.   Trusting in God and His care we can move out and change-Hebrews 11:8.

34.   We need to take responsibility for our own lives instead of focusing and controlling others lives- Matthew 7:3-5.

35.   Anxiety and controlling others are not Godly traits- I Peter 3:8-9; 5:6-11.

Trusting God and His Truth

36.   We are called to trust God- Ps 112:7; Psalm 118:8-9; Psalm 145; Proverbs 13:20; Romans 15:13; Isaiah 2:22.

37.   To learn to trust God instead of being controlling we need to: pray without ceasing (Philippians 4:6), Read the Word (Proverbs 3:5-6), be in community with other believers (Ecclesiastes 4:9-10).

38.   We need to dispense with lies and be transformed by God's truth- Philippians 3:7-21; I John 15-17.

39.   God must be our refuge from our sin and our pain- Psalm 73:21-28; Jude 24, 25.

Sanctification

40.   Seeing how our childhood affected us is the beginning of our recovery but making the decision to seek and cling to God is the hope and meat of our recovery.

41.   God calls us to be made new- Ephesians 4:17-5:20.

42.   God is at work in us. We need to be committed to Him in the process of sanctification- Romans 8:28-39.

43.   God is in charge and He owns our life- Jeremiah 10:23, 24.

44.   We need to know the Word- Romans 12:2.

Godly Relationships

45.   To have Godly relationships, we need to know how God defines love- Romans 12:9-21; Ephesians 4:29-32; 5:21; Philippians 2:1-4; I Corinthians 13:4-13.

THE EBENEZER WOMEN'S MINISTRY OVERVIEW EBENEZER I AND II

Ebenezer is a ministry for women who come from severely dysfunctional/impaired homes where alcoholism, incest and sexual abuse, mental illness, verbal and physical abuse, trauma and neglect were a part of the family system.

I Samuel 7:12 says: "Then Samuel took a stone and set it up between Mizpah and Shen. He named it 'Ebenezer', saying "Thus far the Lord helped us." We call ourselves "Ebenezer" because God is our rock and our help.

Ebenezer I is a series of ten weekly classes. The topics are:

- Our Stories and Our Traits
- Shame and Hiding
- Perfectionism
- Grieving and Mourning
- Forgiving and Letting Go
- New Identity and New Beginning

Ebenezer II is for "graduates" of Ebenezer I and a deeper study consisting of ten classes. Topics are:

- Boundaries
- Loneliness, Trust and Control and The Struggle For Intimacy
- Obsessive-Compulsive Behaviors

- How Our Past Affects Our Marriage
- Conflict and Intimacy In Marriage

These subjects are explored through God's truth and who He says we are as women who struggle with the after affects of our childhood. We seek to find our understanding and healing in our Great Physician.

EBENEZER HAS TWO RULES:

RULE ONE

You have the right to remain silent. No one is required to share or speak at any time and every effort will be made to protect you from being "put on the spot".

RULE TWO

You have the right to confidentiality. What is shared during class is to remain in the class-room. This means refraining from talking about others in the class or revealing who attends the classes. Our intent is to make Ebenezer a safe haven where we can begin to share our real selves with others whose backgrounds are similar. *While Ebenezer is a safer environment for sharing, it is not a perfect one. It must be understood that there is no guarantee that a group member will not break this understanding.*

THE EBENEZER CLASS FORMAT

Ebenezer is both similar and different from a Bible study. We do study the Bible; God's Word and His truth are what we seek to understand and implement as we bring ourselves to Him for healing. Ebenezer is also a support group where we find other women stories, while different from our own, have similarities that have affected us in like ways.

Even though the particulars of our childhood are different, our struggles are much the same. Ebenezer is meant to be a scriptural toolbox where we look closely at the special broken-ness of our sin in response to having grown up in a severely dysfunctional home. We examine our particular traits learned in order to cope and survive, the lies we have believed, and the sinful patterns we have embraced. We learn the truths that God wants us to incorporate into our lives and the healing only He can provide.

CLASS READING ASSIGNMENTS

EBENEZER I

<u>Released From Shame</u>

Sandra D. Wilson, IV Press, 1990

EBENEZER II

<u>Boundaries</u>

Dr. Henry Cloud, Dr. John Townsend, Zondervan, 1992

<u>Secrets To Lasting Love</u>

Gary Smalley, Simon and Schuster, 2000

AUTOBIOGRAPHY IN FIVE SHORT CHAPTERS

I walk down the street.

There is a deep hole in the sidewalk,

I fall in

I am lost…I am helpless

It isn't my fault.

It takes forever to find a way out.

    I walk down the same street.

    There is a deep hole in the sidewalk.

    I pretend I don't see it.

    I fall in again.

    I can't believe I am in the same place,

    But it isn't my fault.

    It still takes a long time to get out.

        I walk down the same street

        There is a deep hole in the sidewalk.

        I see it is there.

        I still fall in. It's a habit.

        My eyes are open.

        I know where I am.

        It is my fault.

        I get out immediately.

            I walk down the same street.

            There is a deep hole in the sidewalk.

            I walk around it.

                I walk down another street.

By Portia Nelson

Repeat After Me, Claudia Black

THE EBENEZER
PROGRAM

EBENEZER I

THE EBENEZER PROGRAM
INTRODUCTION GUIDE FOR TEACHERS

How to Welcome the Class

The Ebenezer classes draw a wide variety of people. Those that make the effort to become a part of the group are motivated by "felt need". Emotional pain, depression, chronic anxiety and confusion about how to live life drive the participants past inertia and into the risk of exposure. The backgrounds of these women are all different and the stories are all unique and important but the underlying pain and need are remarkably similar. The first priority in welcoming a new class, is to provide an atmosphere of safety and kindness. The Ebenezer leader is a guide, not a guru. She doesn't know it all and has not mastered healing. She is someone else who is on the journey.

The materials for the Ebenezer Program, are arranged so that the leader can read through the outline with the class. Class participants can take turns reading sections, but always on a volunteer basis. No one in the class is required to read or share; only to participate as is comfortable for her. The leader acts as a facilitator, keeping the conversation on track and within the class time frame. The class is most effective when run for 1 ½ hours. This gives enough time for the material to be covered with some limited sharing (more sharing as the year progresses and the material is shortened).

This is a suggested way of introducing the class to Ebenezer and also yourself to the class. Establishing this atmosphere of safety and kindness is essential:

"I think it takes an incredible amount of courage to come to a class like this. Beginning to look at the possibility that there were painful circumstances and events in our lives and that they may be affecting us today is not easy. Coming to a class possibly filled with strangers to do it is really hard! I know because I've been in your chair. I think you'll find that the ladies sitting in the chairs to your right and left will not stay strangers long and you'll recognize that, though the details of our stories will be different, we have so much in common."

Suggested Rules for the Class

When I lead a group, I like to provide the following guidelines:

"There are two rules in this class:
1. You have the right to remain silent! No one is EVER required to talk or share anything. I don't want anyone to ever feel "on the spot".

2. You have the right to confidentiality. This should be a safe place. Nothing that is said here should ever leave the room. My husband doesn't know who attends these classes. Please respect each other's privacy."

This is a good time to point out THE EBENEZER WOMEN'S MINISTRY OVERVIEW which contains rules, reading assignments and a recovery poem.

How to Structure the Class

One of the strengths of the program is the bite-sized commitment of ten classes with a break over the holidays to rest and process the information and then coming back together for the remaining ten classes, refreshed and ready to work again. This is an example of one way to structure the Ebenezer Program. You might say the following:

"Ebenezer I is a series of ten classes. We meet every Tuesday except Thanksgiving week. Ebenezer II begins in February and meets for another 10 classes. We finish in April with a lunch out. Graduates of Ebenezer I and II are invited to participate in Ebenezer III which is a support group where we take turns picking topics to discuss, meeting once a month."

Using the Class Outline in this book

The class outline provided in this book is designed to allow some space for note-taking. Class participants can follow along together with the teacher, using this outline and writing in the spaces as insights and personal applications occur.

Home Studies

Home Study questions are provided after each set of class notes and are designed to encourage the class participants to process the class material at home. These exercises are intended for private reflection and are not discussed in class.

Making a Personal Connection with the Participants

In order to connect with the class and help put everyone at ease, it is usually helpful to disclose just a bit of your own story and why you're teaching the class. If you have a recovery story, share just enough to let the class know you are "one of them". Here is what I would share of my story.

"First of all, let's get this straight: I am NOT teaching these classes because I am so 'together', so sanctified, that you should just be like me! I also grew up in a severely dysfunctional home. I had two alcoholic parents and when I was 35, I crashed and burned. I had 3 years of individual counseling and attended a Christian Children of Alcoholics group and finally began the journey of healing and growing up. These classes come from what God has been teaching me and working in my own life."

The Meaning of Ebenezer

Share with the class:

I Samuel 7:12 says: "Then Samuel took a stone and set it up between Mizpah and Shen. He named it Ebenezer, saying, 'This far the Lord helped us'."

Ebenezer literally means "Rock of Help". If you are here, then you are a survivor. You can say, "Thus far the Lord has helped me." even if you didn't know it growing up, or even if you don't know it now.

We can have courage to forge ahead.........because in Christ we have HOPE.

Let's pray and begin.

An Alternate Way To Use This Book

The Ebenezer Program was designed to be used in a group format. Indeed, it has been my experience that this kind of recovery growth is accelerated in a community setting. However, sometimes there is no group available or maybe we are not ready to dive in with both feet and instead need to test the waters a bit first. This book contains all the course material and class outlines with teacher's notes so that an individual can begin study independently if necessary. If you are studying on your own, I would encourage you to find a safe person who has an understanding of family systems and the need for confidentiality, to hear your story. It is in the act of telling what happened to us and where we are with our pain in some kind of community, that we begin to emerge from isolation and find healing. Tread carefully here; not everyone is safe. While it is true that not every licensed counselor is helpful and knowledgeable about family systems, finding a licensed Christian counselor is probably the best place to start. I urge you not to "go it alone". That is usually the way we have approached life from childhood and it is that very isolation that prevents us from the healing God has for us.

EBENEZER I
CLASS 1 AND 2
CLASS OUTLINE WITH TEACHER'S NOTES

I.   All children are raised in "dysfunctional" homes, because all parents are dysfunctional in their sin. But some children are raised in homes where:

1. Most of their needs were disregarded and unmet.
2. Where they were not allowed to function as children; to play, make mistakes, be curious, ACT like children.
3. Where parents became children and the children were forced to parent not only themselves, but their parents as well.
4. Where children were subjected to severe trauma and/or cruelty, physical, emotional, verbal, sexual abuse, lack of safety.

As children, we cope any way we can. We do that in two ways:

1. We block and numb our feelings and reality itself. We live in the gray. When we block the bad feelings, we also block the color and joy of our life.
2. We develop unhealthy and untrue thoughts, feelings and behaviors that help us to survive

II.   The GOOD NEWS is:

1. We survived!
2. We are survivors!
3. We are strong for our experiences and our pain because GOD NEVER WASTES ANY PAIN!

The BAD NEWS is:

1. We carry those coping mechanisms, survival tactics we learned so well into adulthood. They become like heavy packed suitcases that we drag behind us.

2. We carry those unhealthy and untrue thoughts and behaviors over into adulthood BECAUSE that is the only way we know how to live.

Much of how we live today reflects how we adapted as children to our family trauma. These coping mechanisms worked as children but as adults they become burdens and our life just doesn't "work" now. You are probably here because the pain became too great or something in your life wasn't going right.

III.   HOW DID WE ADAPT?

What do I mean by adapt and why is it a problem NOW?

What worked as children no longer works as adults. We are stuck in patterns of behavior that helped us survive as children but sabotage us as adults.

We learned the rules of the family-unspoken, unwritten, but very present in many homes.

The rules are not posted on the refrigerator[1], but we know them well!

The rules in a troubled home all serve to protect the "disequilibrium" of the family.

The over-riding rule is: Don't rock the boat!!

One of the hallmarks of an unhealthy family is that it is static, not dynamic. The roles in the family do not tend to change; someone taking on hero and then changing to clown. There is little or no growth and problem solving. The family is "stuck".

The rules are there to protect the impaired parents from facing their personal problems and to keep from changing. Change and growth are seen as enemies.

When interacting with the outside world, impaired parents model the family's TOP PRIORITY: Looking perfect[2]. What matters most is not how you ARE but how you LOOK.

All the energy of the family is spent in keeping up appearances rather than on real problem solving. So problems DON'T get solved and change and growth are impossible.[3]

So, what are the rules that say "Don't rock the boat"?

1. DON'T TALK

This is the most harmful rule because it keeps us in a prison; there is no room to get better, to get help, because we can't talk.

"Keep the secret" is the BIGGIE.

A woman shared with me, "I don't remember anyone ever saying directly to me, "Don't talk", but I knew the rule quite well. At 19 I married and broke out of the "family system". Apparently I was separated enough that I once mentioned to my uncle a reference to my father's "heavy drinking" and within days I was scolded by a mortified mother. Nobody talked in my extended family that was made up of alcoholics, drug dependants and homosexuals. We all lived the fantasy of the lovely, perfect family. When I first began to say the unspeakable out loud to counselor and support group, I was overcome with feelings of naughtiness and shame.

As adults (this woman was 35 when she started her recovery) we continue the secret keeping, the burying of the truth, trying to survive. BUT THERE IS A PRICE TO PAY!

[TEACHER'S NOTE: Read the following excerpt from <u>The Healing Journey For Adult Children of Alcoholics</u>, by Daryl E. Quick, pg. 34-35]

THE LEAKAGE THEORY

"Surviving childhood can be like stuffing garbage into bags and hiding them in the garage every day. After years of filling bags and stacking them, the garage gets full. We have to compress them to allow for more bags. Some of them break, become untied or wear out. But we still fill the garage with garbage. We notice a smell coming from the garage. Something needs to be done, but we do not know what to do. Still, we squeeze in more garbage. The smell increases. We continue to compress the bags and fill the garage.

"Eventually a black, slimy fluid oozes out of the stack and flows under the door. It travels outside, down the driveway. We clean up the mess. We spray the garage with scents to destroy the smell. It still stinks. We clean again. We stuff more bags. We spray, clean, stuff and become more angry, frustrated and discouraged. "Where will this end?" we ask. We clean up again, filling more bags with garbage. These bags leak more of the dark substance. *Our lives become organized around keeping the stuff in the garage from affecting the beauty and odor of our house. But we cannot keep the bags from leaking.*

Finally we start our recovery process because the pain and hurts can no longer be contained and 'cleaned up'".[4]

Secret keeping runs deep.

[TEACHER'S NOTE: Read the following excerpts from <u>Released From Shame,</u> pages 46-48.]

"I recently read about a dramatic example of the "be quiet" rule's function to protect impaired parents. In a study of fourteen adolescent males on death row, the researchers observed that: Eight of the 14 had injuries severe enough to require hospitalization ….Twelve had been brutally abused and five had been sodomized by relatives. Their parents had a high rate of alcoholism, drug abuse, and psychiatric hospitalization. The boys had tried to conceal all this during their trials. They preferred to be seen as bad rather than admit that they were…victims of ….abuse. *The parents often cooperated with the prosecution (and even urged the death sentence) because they had an interest in concealing their own actions.*

…the more unhealthy the family, the more energy is invested in keeping up appearances (appearance management). …In a family like that, children soon learn how rigid the "be quiet" rule is outside the family. Beth certainly did.

Beth's father was a prominent pastor in a small western community. Beth's father was also physically abusive. If Beth's family had been functioning in an adequate and appropriate manner, her father would have sought help to change when he recognized that he was beginning to express his rage by kicking and punching his children. Beth's mother would have protected her children and confronted her husband. Whether he obtained professional or lay counseling, Beth's father would have been willing to be accountable for practicing strategies designed to change his abusive behavior. Perhaps the entire family would have gone for counseling. At any rate, the emphasis would have been on solving the problem. That's not how Beth remembers the family's focus.

'I used to wonder why my mother was more concerned with my father's reputation and 'ruining the family's testimony in the community' than she was with how much pain I felt. Honestly, there were times when my arms and legs looked like a Picasso. When the bruises were really colorful, the solution was always the same – wear leotards and long-sleeved dresses. (My mother and father were too spiritual to allow girls to ear slacks.) Even during the miserably hot summers, I had to wear long sleeves and thick leotards to hide my bruised arms and legs. I don't really remember being told to keep quiet about Dad's abusiveness. I just knew what was expected of me. Besides, I loved Jesus and sure didn't want to be the one to ruin our family's Christian witness.'"[5]

Secrets are facts hidden in darkness. GOD IS THE Light of revelation and truth. There is no place for this darkness.

[**TEACHER'S NOTE:** Read (taking turns around the room if possible, never calling on anyone directly or forcing reading by all reading in order) :
Psalm 27:1; John 3:19-21; John 1:3-5; I Peter 2:9; Psalm 18:28]

2. DON'T FEEL
In this kind of family the message is clear:
You are NOT afraid
You are NOT unhappy
You are NOT angry

And the consequences of having any real or negative feelings is taught by grievous results... "If you are afraid, unhappy, angry, or feel what I don't want you to feel, then you will make me unhappy; and if I am unhappy, trust me, YOU will be miserable because I will make you miserable!"

The feelings that are natural to a child living in this kind of home are too terrifying and intense to survive and so numbness is learned.

Feelings are indicators of who we are and what we think. When we block our feelings, we lose our sense of who we are and the truth about what we are thinking. There is nothing right or wrong about feelings; they are merely signals to us about what is going on inside us. If we don't know what we are feeling or are afraid to be honest about our feelings with ourselves, we cannot deal with what is wrong with our thinking or our life.

If we fall into the habit of numbing our feelings, we can begin to believe that we can control our feelings by simply shutting them off, refusing them. "If my parents don't want me to feel that way, if it's too terrible for me to feel that, then I simply will not." This becomes habitual, but it is deadly. Somewhere under the numbness our feelings are festering. We are simply stuffing them down inside. And there are consequences for doing this.

3. DON'T TRUST

It is clear that in these kinds of homes, the parents cannot be relied upon. Instead, feelings of safety and trust are replaced with the burden of being on one's own.

4. DON'T THINK

Don't assess, don't see and don't think what we don't want you to think.
One woman reported, "When I was 12, my father held my mother around the neck in the basement, her head against the wood stair post and was stabbing the knife over and over into the wood just inches from her neck. The terror of the moment overpowered all the rules and I went screaming up the stairs. My parent's reactions were typical; my father stayed in the basement, my mother came upstairs and asked, "What's wrong? Everything's fine! You are NOT scared! Your father

LOVES you!" The incident was never discussed and never mentioned again. Their reactions "told" me that the reality I saw never happened……" Don't think.

5. BE GOOD

Never inconvenience parents

Never embarrass or disappoint parents

Never have personal needs

Know how to do everything correctly without being taught; become a master of make-it-up-as-you-go and fake it, fake it, fake it!

Never have a critical or separate thought

Thrive on instability, chaos and pain. Thrive so the family can look perfect!

Never be less than perfect

Do everything parents ask instantly, joyfully, perfectly. This is often the scene in military families.

Never remember and never feel anything except the "happy times" and smile, smile, smile![6]

In other words, do not BE a child. In fact, do not be a person, a normal human being.

Our God was with us even then, though we may have been unaware. We call ourselves Ebenezer because our God has kept us, been with us.

Read II Samuel 22:5-20. He is our HOPE. Read verse 29 and 30.

[TEACHER'S NOTE: This is a good place to target ending the first class. Wherever you end in the outline, announce that next week you will finish the outline and indicate the remaining topics.]

IV. Growing up coping with an unhealthy home environment causes certain traits to develop in reaction to the impaired family. If your family was in trauma, you will identify with many, but not necessarily all:

1.   Feelings numbed (stuffed)-living in the gray. This is a kind of depression. Being aware of and comfortable with feelings is usually NOT a part of our experience. We believe some feelings are acceptable, others are not. So numbed are our feelings that we may not be able to put a label on individual feelings once we begin to experience them.

2.   Denial of reality. "This isn't happening", "He's not like that", "I'm not like that".

3.   Overly intense feelings at inappropriate times. Over-reacting like a volcano, exploding.

4.   Feeling helpless/hopeless. Some level of depression.

5.   Overly fearful of authority figures.

6.   Unable to identify needs and ask for help. As children we were taught to never have needs and no one was there to meet them anyway!

7.   Extremely critical of self. Low self-esteem.

8.   Trouble with intimacy and trust in relationships. We didn't grow up seeing it, we didn't experience it, we don't know how to do it. We are afraid.

9.   Fear of abandonment. This can be a biggie and affect us in so many ways. We may cling and control. We may avoid relationships in order not to be hurt again.

10.   Unable to have fun. Can't let go, need to control, no time after the constant quest for perfection, acceptance.

11.   Compulsive/addictive behavior. This is a form of running and hiding from the pain and the truth.

12.   Crisis oriented living. Crisis diverts the pain and attention from our problem. This was modeled for us in our homes.

13.   Need to control our environment. We are looking for a sense of safety.

14.   Hyper vigilance. This is a finely tuned skill, learned by the necessity of reading our parents faces and moods in order to avoid upsetting them.

15.   Thinking in absolutes/black or white, all or nothing.

16.   Rigid and inflexible.

17.   Physical problems (weight-too much, too little, eating disorders) stomach problems, headaches, nervousness

18.   Perfectionism (the need to be perfect in order to be acceptable) This is so important we will spend an entire week on the topic.

19.   Feelings of shame and guilt. One woman shared that her father ranted most nights when he was drunk that she and her mother had ruined his life. Next week's lesson is about shame.

20.   Loneliness. Feeling isolated and "different".

21.   Confusion about what is "normal". We never knew the word!

22.   Overly responsible for others, losing a sense of "self". Over functioning for everyone.

We can look at these traits and think, "I'm a mess! I hate the way I am! You think my self-esteem was low before-you should see it now!

Before we despair, we need to be careful to look at ourselves through God's eyes. Read Psalm 139:1-16, Psalm 16:5-11. [**TEACHER'S NOTE:** If the group responds, let some of the women read aloud. As always, never call on anyone directly to read.]

V.   If we recognize ourselves in that list of traits and are finding life difficult because we are "stuck" in old patterns, then what do we do?

We need to commit to the truth. The common denominator in any dysfunctional family is secrets and lies, the denial of truth. One former pastor's wife writes,

"When my past caught up with me at age 35, we were living in New Jersey and my husband was to be the speaker at our old church in Maryland for a retreat. I was a weak, fragile, confused physical and emotional mess. I was embarrassed and filled with shame. I wanted to hide and I was afraid to go. Afraid of everything. At the last minute, the fear of staying home alone outweighed the fear of going. For me, though, that self-exposure that I was forced into was the first step of healing."

What is TRUTH and where does it come from? Read Phil 4:8; Ps 25:4-5; Ps 26:2-3; 3 John 3-4; John 14:6

It has been said that , "the truth sets us free, but first it makes us miserable[7]." Recovery is a little like that and that's why so many choose to keep hiding in darkness. But if we choose the truth, the darkness loses its power over us. It's very painful to work through these childhood memories and to begin to feel. "As children, we may have been taught to turn from the truth and evade it[8]." Recovery "begins when we turn toward the truth and embrace it[9]." We find the support and beginnings of intimacy that we missed and so long for. We don't have to be alone anymore.

Feeling alone is a big problem for many of us. There is a difference between isolation and loneliness. Everyone is lonely-this is a condition of our broken-ness. We are meant to be one with our Creator and one another and one day we will be! Isolation, however, is a prison. Isolation is brought about by fear of exposure, fear of imperfection, fear of loss of control, fear of getting close, fear of losing and abandonment. These fears have their roots in wrong thinking and are a spiritual problem. We will explore them all.

There is an old Chinese proverb that says, "If we do not change our direction, we are likely to end up where we are headed[10]."

This class is about challenging old ways of thinking and behaving. Its about changing our direction.

[TEACHER'S NOTE:

At this point the leader has a choice depending on time available (keep to the appointed closing time!) and the mood of the group. If there is time, and the group is interacting freely, the class could be invited to share:

1. What they thought was particularly interesting about this past 2 week topic.
2. What they identified with.
3. Something about their families dysfunction.

Many groups will not be ready yet for this kind of interaction. That's ok. It's more important to end on time and be sensitive to the comfort level of the group. End in prayer.

EBENEZER I
HOME STUDY
CLASS 1 AND 2

[TEACHER'S NOTE: Home Study questions are designed to encourage the class participants to process the class material at home. These exercises are intended for private reflection and are not discussed in class.]

1. Spend some time thinking about your own childhood. What is your story? Have you ever told it to anyone?

2. What "rules" were present in your family? (Don't talk, don't feel, don't trust,. Don't think, be good) What did following those rules mean for you?

3. Look over the list of character traits. Do you identify with any of them? Which ones?

4. How do you feel about the idea of "committing to the truth" and being open to God changing you? If you feel afraid, what scares you the most?

EBENEZER I
CLASS 3 SHAME AND HIDING
CLASS OUTLINE WITH TEACHER'S NOTES

Dealing with shame is an important part of the recovery process and an important part of growing up. When we grow up in an unhealthy home, shame becomes a part of our very core.

Q: What is shame? How do we learn shame?

In her book, *Released From Shame*[1], Sandra D. Wilson suggest that there are three kinds of shame. In order to simplify the picture and help us understand the basis of shame, I have broken the picture into two parts instead of three:

Biological shame and Biblical shame. One is based on truth and one is based on lies.
"***Biblical shame*** is an appropriate, healthy response when we acknowledge that we are different and less than God made us to be and that we are separated from Him by our sin[2]." Isaiah 55:8 says, "For My thoughts are not your thoughts, neither are your ways My ways." Read Heb. 4:12-13.

Wilson[3] says we can respond to Biblical shame in one of three ways:

1. We can deny the separation. Humans eliminate God and elevate human beings to a level of unlimited potential. "We are all basically good."
2. We do not deny our sin nature, but deny that God has provided a bridge over the chasm that separates us from our Creator.

The first sees no need and the second sees no hope.

3.   The third response is to believe that Jesus is the only bridge. John 14:6 says, "I am the way, the truth and the life. No man comes to the Father except through me." Read Romans 5:6-11. Read Romans 7:14-8:2.

Biological shame[4] is something we "catch" from our family. The family rules are impossible to follow perfectly and the inability to be and do these things creates shame. Don't talk. Keep secrets. Secrets themselves can bring a sense of shame. Don't feel. Be good. Do not have personal needs. Do everything perfectly without being taught. Never embarrass, never disappoint. We are doomed to fail and shame is born. A sad example of this is something you often see demonstrated by tense, tired mothers in the grocery store. The child acts like a child by being curious, exuberant, caught up in the fun of the moment and the mother, embarrassed by the childlike behavior, shames her child by scolding him for being in the way, for not being quiet. There is no training her child about the expectations of public behavior, just the sudden and sorry scolding for revealing who he is to others.

The process of learning shame goes something like this[5]:
- Parents/ caregivers project unrealistic expectations on children
- Parents/caregivers consistently distort and deny large chunks of reality in order to conceal addictions, compulsions, chemical dependencies, workaholism
- Children see parents/caregivers as perfect with appropriate expectations-good children are perfect children without developmental limitations and legitimate childhood needs. Perfect children would be able to perfectly please. That is the lie that creates shame.
- We keep failing, failing, failing.

S. Wilson[6] has a wonderful analogy that vividly portrays the process of learning shame. She likens the phenomenon to the interlocking ability of Velcro:

- "Hooking the Shame"- Velcro has two sides: loops and hooks. In overtly and subtly abusive families, parents use shaming to control their children. Parents plant shame loops by creating unrealistic expectations and distorting reality. Requiring the children to obey the family rules and keep up the perfect family façade creates the shame loops that exert control over the children. Then the " shame hooks are perfectly fitted to the pre-existing shame loops" and the resulting bond gives new meaning to "the tie that binds[7]".

[**TEACHER'S NOTE:** It may be helpful to bring a sample of Velcro to the class to illustrate the loops and hooks.]

The loops are the belief system and the hooks are the verbal and non-verbal messages by the caregivers.

- Examples of shaming: Negative comparisons
- Ex.: Declarations of shame-"I'm so ashamed of you. You are such a disappointment. If only you hadn't been born[8]."
- Ex.: Redefining respect-Respect means do everything we say and ask no questions. Any attempt to separate appropriately from parents and develop own individuality defined as disrespecting elders[9].
- Ex.: Praising without affirmation- focusing on performance, not personhood. You may experience yourself not as a "human being", but as a "human doing[10]".

THE VELCRO FAMILY:

The caregivers implant the loop with rules and belief system-a belief system that is:
  1. Based on lies
  2. Developed in order for the caregivers to continue in their addiction
  3. Designed to keep the "secret".
  4. Designed to keep the family static-no change, no growth.

Here are the rules: THE LOOP
  1. Don't be less than perfect
  2. Keep the family rules perfectly.
  3. Don't be an individual.
  4. Don't be different from US.
  5. Do everything we say without question.
  6. Do it my way or else.
  7. You have no intrinsic worth as a person created by God.

The caregiver's day to day verbal and non-verbal messages create the hook that catches us in shame and is used to control us: THE HOOK

  1. "Why can't you be more like Judy?" Comparing twin sisters unfavorably.
  2. Looks of disgust.
  3. Declarations of shame, "I'm so ashamed of you." "You should be ashamed of yourself."
  4. "How could you?" "We always…." If you are your own person then you are shameful.
  5. "Mommy loves you when….you clean up your toys." Performance based acceptance and praise fosters shame. Parent's competitiveness in athletics (Second place is no place) can be a hook[11].
  6. And the really bad news is this: The baton is passed on from generation to generation. We accept our shame and pass it to our children unless we learn truth.

Both Biblical and Biological shame have to do with "different and less-than[12]" status.

1. "In Biological shame, the difference in developmental capacities of children are compared unfavorably with those of adults[13]" and also compared with a mythological perfection. This is the impossible standard that fosters shame.

2. "In Biblical shame, the difference is the essential nature of God in contrast to that of human beings[14]." We do not measure up, we cannot keep the Law so we feel shame.

"The solution to Biblical shame is Grace[15]." Rom. 8:1-4

The solution to Biological shame is Truth and growth.

Psalm 34 holds the answer to both Biological and Biblical shame. Read Psalm 34.

EBENEZER I
HOME STUDY
CLASS 3

1. Where do you stand with Biblical shame? What is your response?

2. What kind of shame "Velcro" was used in your family? Can you think of specific examples of being shamed?

3. When you ponder the family rules, (Don't be less than perfect, Don't be an individual, etc.) which ones do you still feel bound to follow? How does that affect you and your life today?

EBENEZER I
CLASS 4
SHAME AND HIDING, PERFECTIONISM
CLASS OUTLINE WITH TEACHER'S NOTES

I. What is perfectionism?

    Guilt focuses on actions, but shame focuses on identity.

    Perfectionism is an identity crisis that is driven by shame.

    "Perfectionism is an unhealthy pattern of thoughts and behaviors we use to conceal our perceived flaws[1]." These are all the areas we deem to be less than perfect, still believing we are expected to be perfect and feeling shame when we are not.

    Perfectionism is self-protection and shame-based.

    We wrap perfectionism around us in order to protect ourselves.

    How does perfectionism differ from excellence?

    Perfectionism is driven by shame, fear, and pride.

    Excellence is God's abilities and God's strength for God's purposes.

    It is the difference between operating with a full cup or an empty one, and having right or wrong motivation.

II. Perfectionism is a façade. It is about believing and building a false self and a false identity.

    There are two kinds of perfectionists: rookie and veteran. For the rookie, everything is life and death, must-win, equally important. The veteran, however, wants to, actually MUST be perfect but without looking perfectionistic. This is the "really perfect" façade[2]!

III. Perfectionism is a control issue. If we believe we must be perfect, then we
    must control everything about us and around us. If we want to be a veteran, we must
    control HOW we control everything!
    We have to make it look good; "I'm not controlling-I just must have everything
    under control!"

IV. What is the root of perfectionism?
    A. Wrong thinking and believing lies
    B. Fear of exposure

Three important and often-asked questions are:

1. What are we believing that is a lie?
2. Why do we fear exposure?
3. How does this show up in our lives?

In the past, we were laughed at, ridiculed, neglected, abused , and shamed with disgust when our faults and mistakes were exposed. There was abuse and secret- keeping, lies and mixed messages causing us to believe that there must be something wrong with me, I must be a bad person, I am unlovable. We were rewarded for looking perfect. We felt (feel) safer when we can line everything up in us and around us. Life becomes about fear and control, success and approval, hiding and facades.

This is an exhausting, energy sapping way to live!

Sandra Wilson[3] says, "Perfectionism is a bottomless pit of demands and disappointments because you can never satisfy its specifications"

Some ladies have sat back, with some relief, and said, "Well, at least I don't have THAT problem! You should see my house!"

However, the fear that drives perfectionism can show up in our lives in two different ways: Aggressive or Passive.

Aggressive:

1. Bragging and attention seeking, pride replacing insecurity.
2. Sarcastic, bitter, biting, competitive
3. Living a driven life, worshiping at the idol of Perfect. Pushing to succeed and be approved by others. "All my life I climbed the ladder of success only to find it leaning against the wrong wall!" Driven and unable to relax, medicating the nagging fear that I am not yet acceptable with chronic striving and activity.

Passive: Withdrawn and emotionally absent

Depressed and defeated, still believing the lie that I must be perfect but knowing that I can't. Acquiescent, "whatever....", "I can't be perfect so I'm no good and I give up."

V. What is the lie and the truth about perfectionism?

The "lie promotes the fantasy that this is a perfect world populated with perfect people[4]" so that I must be perfect or else I don't belong, I won't be acceptable.

The truth is that this is a broken world filled with broken and imperfect people. We are sinful; only God is perfect. We fit in "imperfectly" with everyone else[5].

"Inherent in our sin natures is the deep sense that something in us is missing and not quite right[6]." This truth becomes confused with our biological shame, our fear, and our need to control. Instead of seeing the difference between Biblical shame and biological shame, and accepting God's way of dealing with our real sin, we have exchanged the truth of God for a lie. (Rom. 3:9-28) We attempt to create our own self-righteous solution: "I will be perfect, pretend I'm perfect, deny I'm not perfect, hide my imperfections from others and...even myself[7]."

And if I am "found out", I will feel shame.
This is pride and the idol of self.
Read Jer. 2:13

The Gospel alone has the truth and power to heal. We are fully exposed before a loving, gracious and compassionate God. Perfection is in, and comes only from God.
Read Psalm 18:30-32, Psalm 25:1-7, Phil. 3:1-14; Romans 3: 9-20

VI. The fear that drives perfectionism is NOT from God. Read Psalm 27.

VII. The question is: If I am not that façade of the perfect person, then who am I? What do we do after that terrible moment of panic and identity crisis?

> If I let go of the quest for control and perfectionism, let go of the façade of "perfect", then it feels like a free-fall over a cliff!

This point is the point of "growing up" and the beginning of "freedom"- freedom to learn who God made us to be and who we are in Him. There is freedom from carrying around those old trunks of pain and those old lies that have dogged us once we decide to give up the idol of perfectionism and seek God.

How is perfectionism an idol? Read Isaiah 44:15, 17, 20, 21, 22
What does it mean to seek God? Gal. 2:20

VIII. Remember: It is easier to relinquish perfectionistic behavior than perfectionistic beliefs. Only by giving up the beliefs that are at the root of perfectionism can we begin to change. God looks on our heart[8].

Read Gal. 3:1-5

[TEACHER'S NOTE: End with Psalm 23-When the Lord is our Shepherd, we lack nothing.]

EBENEZER I
HOME STUDY
CLASS 4

1. Are you caught in perfectionism? How does that affect your life? Be specific.

2. Which camp do you find yourself in: Aggressive Perfectionism or Passive Perfectionism? What does that look like in your life?

3. What fear do you think drives your perfectionism?

EBENEZER I
CLASS 5 AND 6 - GRIEVING AND MOURNING
CLASS OUTLINE WITH TEACHER'S NOTES

[**TEACHER'S NOTE:** The end point between classes 5 & 6 is flexible. An additional outline for Class 6 follows.]

I. What is grief?

Grief is a normal response to loss. It is a process whereby deep feelings aroused by loss are acknowledged and fully expressed[1].

In "successful grieving", the mourner gradually becomes able to make attachments and investments in other persons, things[2].

What does grief look like?

Grief can manifest itself in a pre-occupation with lost person or thing.
There are intense feelings of guilt, shame, terror, bewilderment, emptiness, sadness, despair, and helplessness.
There can be bodily distress.

But why are we talking about grieving?

1. Every human being has losses, so if we are human, grieving is a necessary part of life.

2. Growing up in a dysfunctional, abusive family creates greater pain and more losses than the more healthy family.

3. Children from dysfunctional homes do not know how to grieve. They have not been allowed or taught how to grieve so the terrible sadness is buried and continues to grow.

What are the losses in this life? In <u>Healing Journey</u>[3], Daryl Quick, describes just how pervasive are these losses.

1. "Important Person – death, separation, divorce, rejection, illness, children leaving.

2. Physical Loss – part of one's body, an accident, an image of body which does not match cultural expectations, self-esteem, sexual or physical abuse.

3. Childhood – not having healthy parents, loss of early objects of attachment (toys, pet), low status in the family, separation, divorce, chaos, trauma.

4. Adult Loss – jobs, relationships, dreams or goals, health, transitions, mistakes, victimized by burglary, assault.

5. Material Loss – objects of value, money, property, sentimental object and collections"

[TEACHER'S NOTE: A diagram page is provided at end of this outline. Take 5 minutes of class time to allow each group member individually to begin their chart. Encourage the class to complete the chart at home. Plan for a brief time at the beginning of the next class for sharing of insights gained through the process.]

Children from impaired homes don't know how to grieve.

Don't talk. Don't feel. Don't think. Don't have needs. The rules of the family do not leave room for grieving. Adults from impaired homes are usually carrying a suitcase full of pain around. Life on earth is about loss- life is change. There is loss of youth, loss of health, independence, loss of friends, family, and spouse through death and divorce.

For someone from impaired parents, there is also the loss of childhood, the loss of the fantasy of the perfect parents, the perfect family, the loss of being able to "fix" the family's problems. There is the grief of unmet needs from childhood coupled with the inability as an adult to identify, feel and successfully meet needs.

No wonder we have grieving and mourning to do!

Sometimes the Christian community has trouble with the concept of grieving.
1. Grieving means not accepting
2. Grieving means not being joyful
3. Hurry up-you're making me uncomfortable. Aren't you through yet?

II. What happens when we don't grieve our losses?

When there are unspoken and unaddressed losses from childhood left "un-grieved", life's current losses grow out of proportion. We are less able as adults to grieve everyday losses and move on in our life.

1. Stuffing our grief takes a terrible toll-
2. It requires vast amounts of energy
3. It causes depression
4. Sometimes "requires" self-medicating: food, alcohol, drugs, sleep, sex, shopping
5. Numbs all our feeling- we live life in the gray.

Must we go through this step of mourning and grieving for real recovery to take place?

Why do we avoid it?
   1. Fear of our feelings
   2. Fear of the "bottomless pit"
Fear is the big word here!

Isaiah 49:8-26; II Corinthians. 1:3-7 tell us of God's faithfulness and comfort in our restoration.

III. How do we learn to grieve?

   1. Know it is good to grieve our losses. Christians sometimes think it is wrong to grieve. Grieving is a spiritual, healthy process built in by God. John 11:33-36; Psalm 88.

2. Recognize the stages of grief. Study some persons in the Bible as they grieve. Denial- this is not happening to me Anger- Why? That's not fair! Bargaining—if only I had.. Give me another chance. Depression—nothing matters anymore. Acceptance-letting go and a new beginning[4].

3. Identify the physical feelings that accompany grief- Tightness in throat choking, shortness of breath, sighing, empty feeling in the abdomen, lack of muscle power, headaches, insomnia, loss of appetite and weight, fatigue, dizziness, indigestion[5].

Use tools to help yourself:

1. Work with a counselor with knowledge of family systems
2. Keep a journal of your feelings.
3. Fill your head with TRUTH- do Bible studies on topic of grieving, sorrow and God's comfort. Study the book of Job.
4. Know that the intense feelings will NOT kill you and they will pass.

IV. Two Kinds of Grieving

1. Responsibility without grief[6] (forget the past, move on, forgive and forget) This would be so tidy, so clean and easy if only we could pull it off! The Church today is filled with people being "overly responsible" and doing all the " shoulds" and "oughts" imposed or perceived in order to be accepted.
Notice the motivation: "to be accepted". Doing, not out of obedience, love and response to Christ, with a full cup, but instead, in order to be accepted, approved of, or loved by other people.
Every loss is met emotionless, the smile is a façade and there is the ever-present drive to "do more".

2. Grief without responsibility[7]. The grieving process can be overwhelming. There are feelings of shock, self-pity, anger, extreme hurt and the feeling of being victimized. The process of grieving and mourning is an important one because the feelings are genuine and many of us were , in fact, victims.

BUT! If we do not move through this stage, we will be stuck in grief. Stuck feeling angry and sorry for ourselves. Stuck blaming others.

You were a victim, but you do not have to remain a victim. You are an adult and you can take responsibility for pursuing healing and wholeness.

So, there are two ways of getting stuck in grieving:

1. One by avoiding the work of grieving and stuffing the feelings so that we carry the grief all our lives.
2. One by never moving through the work, just camping out for life.

Both involve the idol of "self". I can avoid the work out of fear and the need for approval instead of trusting the Great Physician to heal me and use me for His Kingdom. I can focus the rest of my life on how I was victimized, how I hurt, again not trusting the Great Physician to heal me and use me for His Kingdom, every old and new loss met with anger and self-pity and added to the "pack".

V. If we are ready to "grow up", here are some of the new thinking and behaviors (note thinking comes first!) we can practice:

1. Feel our feelings instead of suppressing them. Sounds simple but can be desperately hard to do, especially at the beginning.

2. Talk about our family secret in appropriate settings instead of hiding or denying it.

3. Think about long-buried events. Use old photos to work your way through the events.

4. Stop fixing others by trying to make them happy, successful, good.

5. Start taking care of our own needs too.

6. Develop trust instead of fear. God is trustworthy so we can start taking small steps of believing He will not leave us, He will keep us safe.

7. Tell people the truth. First tell ourselves the truth!

8. Set boundaries in relationships. More on that in Ebenezer II.

9. Have fun instead of feeling guilty for relaxing. Practice this with a fun friend!

10. Stop being driven; slow down. This helps us stop medicating our pain so that we can "feel the feelings", start being honest and start moving through the grieving work.

11. Set a budget and stick to it. Another way to medicate pain is overspending.

12. Tell others what we want instead of making them guess. More in Ebenezer II.

13. Ask others what they mean instead of mind reading. Learn to pursue truth.

14. Stop exaggerating. This connects with the black and white, all or nothing thinking that is a part of our over-reacting.

15. Take the initiative to be a friend instead of remaining passive. This involves turning our eyes away from ourselves and trusting God when He says we are lovable.

16. Stop to reflect on and correct behavior. But first be aware of what wrong thinking is behind the problem behavior!

17. Quit rationalizing or being defensive when wrong. Seek the truth and trust God that you are lovable. The truth is you're not perfect!

18. Acknowledge cravings, fears, shames, bitterness and hatred. God already knows!

19. Grieve losses instead of denying them. Do the grief work[8]!

LIST PAST LOSSES

_____

_____

_____

LIST CURRENT LOSSES

_____

_____

_____

_____

_____

_____

_____

_____

_____

_____

BELOW, CREATE A TIMELINE OF LOSSES WITH YOUR APPROXIMATE AGE AT THE TIME OF EACH LOSS:

Birth ---**Today**

_____

EBENEZER I
CLASS 6 GRIEVING AND MOURNING (continued)
CLASS OUTLINE WITH TEACHER'S NOTES

Grieving is the process in which our attachment to the lost person, object, or inner reality are not entirely given up, but are sufficiently altered to permit us to

1. admit the reality of our loss

2. live without constant reference to it

3. restore trust and convictions, though perhaps altered.

Discuss:

1. "The refusal to grieve the disappointments of childhood, to bury them once and for all, condemns us to live in their shadows."

2. "Genuine grief is the sobbing and wailing that expresses the acceptance of our helplessness to do anything about the losses."

3. "We must detach from the past to make room for the present."

Question: Do you think there is a difference between "identifying" our feelings and "having" our feelings?

What do you think of this statement: "We need to EMBRACE those feelings in grief, that is, let them become as big as they really were back then. We need to SHARE those feelings with others, not just TALK about them with others."

Read II Corinthians. 4:16-18. What perspective does this give?

Read Psalm 42. How is this a picture of grieving? What does this psalm model for us doing grief work?

EBENEZER I
HOME STUDY
CLASS 5 AND 6

1. How do you feel about the idea of grieving your childhood?

2. Do you think you have started the process of grieving? Why or why not?

3. What do you think you have to grieve?

4. What do you plan to do in order to help yourself in the grieving process?

EBENEZER I
CLASS 7 AND 8 FORGIVING AND LETTING GO
CLASS OUTLINE WITH TEACHERS NOTES

Forgiveness is one of the most challenging topics that we will face on the road to recovery. These issues are the ones that must be faced.

I.   Why forgive?

II.   Why is forgiveness so hard?

III.   What forgiveness is not

IV.   What forgiveness is

V.   How do we know if we have not truly forgiven?

I. Why forgive? God tells us to forgive

It hurts US not to forgive

        a) Physically, Psalm 32:3-4

        b) Emotionally, we get "stuck" in certain stages of grief such as anger

        c) Healing comes only through forgiving

If we are going to "move on", we must learn to forgive.

II. Why is forgiveness so hard?

In her novel, <u>The Secret Life of Bees</u>, Sue Monk Kidd said "People, in general, would rather die than forgive. It's THAT hard. If God said in plain language, 'I'm giving you a choice. Forgive, or die,' a lot of people would go ahead and order their coffin."

1. We have a tendency to intellectualize the process- We think what we need to do. We think that because we thought the thought, we are done. The thought becomes real through feelings and actions.

   Forgiveness is part of the grieving and mourning process.

2. Fear that the person will hurt us again if we forgive-a pushing away for protection through not forgiving. Fear of becoming enmeshed again-If we forgive, they will have power over us again.

3. We are sinful people-forgiveness is of God

III. What forgiveness is NOT.

1. Minimizing what was done to us. "It wasn't so bad. Others had it worse. They didn't mean it. They did the best they could so it shouldn't hurt." If we do this, we rush through forgiveness.

2. Taking the blame on ourselves-"I deserved it." We were taught this growing up.

3. Something we rush into because:
   - Fear of getting stuck in mourning and grieving-thinking that mourning, grieving, anger are "bad".
   - Fear of the mourning and grieving process and fear of feelings. Fear of the "black hole." I'll never stop crying, the pain will kill me.
   - Other people "rushing us through" mourning and grieving. Everyone is different and has their own timetable

   NOTE: the 2 big mistakes:
   - Forgiving too quickly
   - Not forgiving at all

IV. What forgiveness IS.

1. An "unnatural act". Philip Yancey said all the laws of nature and economics are based on attitudes of eat or be eaten and take what you can get.

2. A choice.

3. No longer viewing our offenders through the eyes of the offense and developing a broader vision of the acts and the person who committed them. This is NOT the same as belittling your own suffering.

4. No longer looking for retaliation-Luke 6:32-36. Obviously, this is a SPIRITUAL act.

5. Breaking the cycle of blame and pain.-Luke 6:37-38. The blame game hurts only you.

6. Releasing those who hurt us, as Christ did, because they did not know what they were doing. If we release them, they can no longer have power over us.

7. Recognizing that we are no different-all of us need forgiveness. The ability to forgive comes from experiencing forgiveness ourselves for our sins toward God and others. We cannot forgive until we are forgiven. How does this fact make others outside of Christ handicapped? Eph. 4:32-5:2.

8. A process-God is patient and kind toward us. He knows how much we can bear and metes out new perceptions as we grow in our ability to handle them. There are usually layers of hurt and anger. The wounds are often deeper than we originally thought.

9. Something that may or may NOT change the persons who wronged us. They may soften or they may harden toward us. We do NOT forgive in order to "get"-that is not forgiveness, but manipulation.

V. How do we know if we have not truly forgiven?

1. Feelings of hurt and anger continue

2. Bitterness in our attitude toward life and others; blaming, not nurturing.

3. Dwelling on the past.

4. No growth in our life; feeling stuck in our list of character traits

5. Displaced anger- controlling anger eventually leads to a reservoir of hatred and rage that explodes in other places, at other people.

6. Hating God, feeling God can't be trusted, blaming God.

All of these can be a part of the grieving and mourning process that must be experienced before forgiving and letting go.

VI. What is essential before we can begin to forgive?

1. Thorough naming of losses and grieving. Thorough=extensive, not complete, because there are layers. We can forgive all we can see; later we may see more.

2. Experiencing forgiveness ourselves for our sins toward God and others. We can't forgive if we still feel like victims, if we are stuck in the grieving and mourning process. (Grief without responsibility) "Look what they did to me" must become "Look what I did to others and toward God". Luke 7:36-50; Matt. 6:9-15. How do these verses relate to our family?

Matt. 18:21-35- Draw the weight of our offenses toward God in relation to other person's offenses toward us using a scale and your imagination.[1]

[TEACHER'S NOTE: Take a few minutes and let some share what they came up with.]

List those persons you may need to forgive.

[TEACHER'S NOTE: Depending on available time, give some quiet time to complete this. Encourage the class to talk about what listing these people felt like and how difficult it was to do.]

VII. What about restitution?

Forgiveness means releasing others from the debt of the wounds they have inflicted. Forgiveness creates a renewed opportunity to base relationships on integrity, mutual respect, and health. But often our "boat rocking" will be a threat to the offender who is still busy denying and burying the secrets. "Forgiveness does not necessitate restitution[2]." Forgiveness provides a platform for restitution but no guarantee of relationship[3].

Luke 6:27-45. The motivation is love, not manipulation.

What might we want to manipulate the other person to do?

EBENEZER I
HOME STUDY
CLASS 7 AND 8

1. Who do you need to forgive? Make a list.

2. What does forgiving that person (persons) mean to you? How do you go about forgiving them? What makes that hard for you?

3. What outcome do you expect if you forgive these people?

4. What signs do you see that you have not truly forgiven those people on your list?

EBENEZER I
CLASS 9 AND 10
YOUR TRUE IDENTITY - A NEW BEGINNING
CLASS OUTLINE WITH TEACHERS NOTES

When we've acknowledged our problem, told our story, faced our issues grieved and mourned the bulk of our issues and learned to forgive and let go where do we go from here?

1. **Continue to face our problems and seek the truth.** Remember the word "process". God is pleased with the process. Our walk of faith with Him is not one that focuses on the end result, but instead courageous strides of trust with Him.

2. **Develop a new identity.** Learn and meditate and practice who we are in Christ's eyes. We need to renew our thinking by learning what God says and change our self-image from "mistake" to "masterpiece".

3. **Learn to feel again.** Take risky flights out of "numbness". Begin to identify and be aware of feelings as they happen. Learn to express your feelings in healthy ways.

4. **Take responsibility for ourselves-become an adult!** We weren't responsible for what happened to us as children (though we often felt as though we were) but we ARE responsible for the actions we take as adults.

5. **Learn what it means to "parent ourselves" and learn to trust God to be our loving Father.**

6. **Identify and remove escape behaviors.** These are deep, learned patterns for escaping truth and pain. It is the behavior of denial learned from our family's pain and modeled for us by our parents. These escape behaviors are destructive:
   • They keep us from healing and health

- They may bring relief at first, but are always followed by remorse, loss of self-respect and a sense of helplessness
- They are self-destructive: bulimia, anorexia, drugs both legal and illegal, alcohol, over-spending, over-sleeping, misused sex, driven over-activity. Satan is the Destroyer, God is the Physician.

7. **Begin to learn to trust and connect with others.** Small steps, safe people. Learn about boundaries. Our class and Ebenezer III support group are excellent ways to practice this in a safe environment.

8. **Learn to ask for what we need.** This is part of taking responsibility for ourselves and becoming an adult.

9. **And the equally important flip side of this is: Learn to let go of what we cannot get.** We have the habit of needing to control others and our environment in order to escape pain and difficult emotions-in other words, in order to escape our recovery work! Learning to identify our needs and ask for them is a beginning; learning that sometimes we need to let go and accept NOT having a need met is as important as the first step.

10. **Celebrate our victories.** If we were raised in an impaired home, our day often consists of surviving, avoiding and escaping. As we work through recovery, there are moments where we learn what it's like to be truly alive, where we can feel joy and freedom from our baggage. See the positive, the GOOD that God produces through our pain:
- He develops character in us
- We learn to comfort others with the comfort that was given to us

11. Comfort others.

Read Psalm 30. How is the Lord described as our "Ebenezer" (rock of help) in this psalm?

- You turned my wailing into dancing.
- You lifted me out of the depths.
- You brought me out of the grave.
- You clothed me with joy.

Read Psalm 103. What good things does the Lord give us?

- Forgives
- Love and compassion
- Gracious to us
- Heals
- Satisfies
- Renews
- Redeems
- Reveals
- Righteousness and justice

EBENEZER I
HOME STUDY
CLASS 9 AND 10

1. Where do you think you are now in the process of recovery?

2. If you haven't started journaling yet, commit to try it today.

3. How comfortable are you with having feelings instead of being numb? Name the feelings you experienced today if you can.

4. What behaviors do you practice in order to escape feelings and pain (and ultimately your recovery!)?

5. Choose a passage of Scripture on which to meditate and memorize during the winter break from class. Find one that speaks to you and is a special encouragement.

THE EBENEZER
PROGRAM

EBENEZER II

EBENEZER II
CLASS 1 AND 2
BOUNDARIES, SELF-ESTEEM AND CO-DEPENDENCY
CLASS OUTLINE WITH TEACHERS NOTES

Growing up in impaired, sometimes traumatic households, gives us little idea about who we are and how we relate to others. Where do others end and I begin? The concept of having personal boundaries that define us as people may have never entered our thoughts.

1. What are boundaries? Are they good? Are they bad? Do we want them?
2. Boundaries define us. What is me? What is not me[1]?
3. Healthy boundaries help us keep good in and bad out[2].
4. Healthy boundaries are not walls-they are fences with gates in them[3].
   I John 1:9- Let pain and sin OUT (by confession)
   II Corinthians. 6:11-13-Open up to give and receive the good.

Coming from abuse causes us to reverse boundaries-we let the bad in and keep the good out. We build walls that have no gates. Or we have no boundaries at all. We might have no real sense of self, separate from others[4].

We let secrets, depression and shame in, keeping intimacy and love outside. We lack the ability to trust.

Why does coming from a severely dysfunctional home give us so much trouble with boundaries?

- Healthy boundaries were not modeled for us-we never saw them!
- Our boundaries were continually transgressed; sexual, physical and emotional abuse are harsh examples of another transgressing our boundaries. Shaming

and the rules of the family (don't be separate, don't think, don't feel, and don't need) define a boundary-less person.

- Separateness was not allowed. To have boundaries by definition is to be a unique, separate person.

So what might our boundaries look like?

- **No boundaries**-no sense of being abused or being abusive (others controlling, rescuing, and abusing us, or, we ourselves controlling, abusing, and rescuing others.) Picture an open field with no property demarcations. This way of not respecting boundaries sadly shows up most clearly in how we relate to our own children. Instead of no boundaries, we may have damaged boundaries; at certain times and to certain individuals we can say "no", set limits and take care of ourselves. There is partial awareness of other's boundaries. But some relationships "push our buttons" and our boundaries dissolve or we may transgress the boundaries of particular people.

- **Walls instead of boundaries**. This is the place we often go when we first discover boundaries. We don't want to STAY in this place! It's a wall with no gates-walls made up of anger and/or fear. We may be closed up, walled off emotionally. Inside our wall we are cut off from other people.

- **Alternating between walls and non-existent boundaries**. We risk vulnerability with no boundaries, becoming that open field, get hurt, and then quickly put up walls. It's all or nothing and the dance is the "Lunatic Fringe Swing".

Families where the parents are alcoholic, emotionally or physically abusive, substance abusive, negligent, co-dependant (meaning that their own personhood is defined by their addiction and their control over the people around them) teach the delusion that the bad feelings can be dealt with by winning the approval of others. The members think "If we (the children in the family) are perfect, the caretakers will stop drinking, abusing, neglecting, etc. and we will be free from the shame, fear, sadness, anger." This gives these people tremendous power over us and unconsciously makes them responsible for our happiness. This drive to win the approval of others develops a powerful need within us to manipulate and control those around us into giving us their approval. And then this becomes a life-long habit and pattern of relating to others unless it is addressed.

When this happens, there is little or no sense of personhood developed within us. The focus is on the other person to feel better about themselves, the other person to make us feel better about our own self. Our personhood is defined by how they are doing and how **they** feel **we** are doing.

Q. How is this people-pleasing/co-dependent way of relating to others different from real love and Godly service to others? Read Gal. 6:7-10

Q. What does the saying, "I live for an audience of one" mean? Do we live like that?

Both these questions bring up the idea of *focus*. We are to "sow to please the Spirit." We "do good" for God, not in order to win favor and acceptance of other people.

5. "The concept of boundaries comes from the very nature of God. God defines himself as a distinct, separate being and He is responsible to Himself. He defines and takes responsibility for His personality by telling us what He thinks, feels, plans, allows, does not allow, likes and dislikes[5]." He is " separate from His creation and from us…. He confronts sin and allows consequences for behavior. He guards His house and does not allow evil to go in there. He invites people to love Him and He allows love to flow[6]" out.

    [TEACHER'S NOTE: At this point, divide the group into smaller groups of 3-5 depending on the total size of group. Challenge each group to find Bible verses that illustrate the healthy boundaries that God models for us.

    Suggest they start with: Isaiah 55:8; Deut. 5:29; Hebrews 12:7-11; Ezekiel 16:58; Proverbs 3:12; Job 5:17; I John 4:1-3]

6. When we are "making boundaries", what is our responsibility to others? How can we love others while making healthy boundaries for ourselves? We are called to love others. I John 4:7 implores us to love one another. Figuring out just where my responsibility to others and my own need to be healthy begins and ends can be a real struggle. If we grew up in a family of damaged boundaries, or maybe no boundaries at all, and if our learned way of relating to others is to try to please and manipulate them to make ourselves feel good, how will we know how to love others in a healthy way?

    "We are responsible TO others and FOR ourselves[7]."
    Read Galatians 6:2-5.
    "Carry each other's burdens", verse 2 means to shoulder each others HEAVY LOADS, burdens too heavy for that person to bear. The language is the same as "bearing the heavy judgment of God"

"Carry your own load", verse 5 means to shoulder your own pack, knap sack, lighter load of daily toil. The language indicates a small light load of a peddler.

When another's load is too heavy to bear, if it is within our God-given strength and ability to do so, we are called to love one another by helping. But we are also reminded to let others carry their own packs instead of being "overly responsible" for others in a pattern of rescuing that doesn't respect their boundaries or our own[8]. Later we'll address control issues that can cause us to confuse our responsibilities with other people's "loads".

7. Why is "no" such a difficult word for us to say? What kind of trouble does that get us into as we relate to others? As Dr. Henry Cloud and Dr. John Townsend put forth in their excellent book, Boundaries, fear is a big factor in our reluctance to say the two-letter word:

- Fear of being selfish, unspiritual. Old tapes and old lies still echo in our minds; we may have been told we were selfish growing up whenever we exhibited any selfhood.
- Fear of losing control of manipulation of others to approve and validate us.
- Fear of other people's anger, shaming us, punishment, and disappointment; after all, "no" is a confrontational word.
- Fear of loss of relationship, abandonment, aloneness; we will say "yes" at any cost. The more codependent we are, and the less healthy our boundaries are, the more we have to lose by saying "no" because we are counting on their approval.
- Fear that we will be mean and selfish if we hold others responsible for their own feelings, choices, and actions. We might be believing that consequences are bad and we are responsible for the consequences of others. Proverbs 13:18-24

- Fear that if we don't rescue, something terrible will not only happen to "them", but to us as well. Proverbs 15:10.

Notice the common word in all of the above: FEAR!

Read Proverbs 29:25, I John 4:18, Psalm 27:1-2

This is a spiritual problem; in Him, we have nothing to fear.

We have a choice over how we relate to others:

- We can let them manipulate us into giving more than we want or CAN give (which leads to resentment, exhaustion, and burn-out).
- Or, we can spend ourselves for others as God directs and gives us strength and resources.

Read Phil. 2:1-18-we are called to a life of love and servant hood. We are not to look only TO OUR OWN INTERESTS (so this *is* part of what we do) but only AFTER finding encouragement, comfort, fellowship, tenderness and compassion from being united with Christ, THEN we are to have the same love, looking to the interests of others.

Read II Corinthians 9:6-15. God is able to make all grace abound to you, so that in all things at all times (when we are full of His grace) HAVING ALL THAT YOU NEED, you will abound in every good work.

Both passages have to do with giving out of a full cup. When we give what God directs us to give, He fills our cup to overflowing. We open our hands and it spills out to others.

How different is this from giving because others have manipulated us, we feel guilty, we need others to approve of us, or we are afraid?

8. We are responsible for our own "pack".

- We are responsible for our own choices; they are ours to make. We cannot say, "I had to", "She made me". We make the choices and we endure or enjoy the consequences[9].
- We are responsible as adults for our values (to what we assign worth, to rate importance[10]). Do we adopt our parent's values? Do we let others choose our values? Or do we choose God's values as our own? Do we even KNOW what God's values are?? Psalm 119:20-24, Jeremiah 9:23-24.
- We are responsible to God. Jeremiah 10:23-24.
- We are responsible for setting limits on others; how they affect and influence us. We can "close the gate", remove ourselves from the situation, and refuse contact. Matthew 18:15-17; I Corinthians 5:9-13; Matthew 10:11-14.

HOME STUDY
EBENEZER II
CLASS 1

1. As you think about boundaries, how would you describe your own?

2. How were your personal boundaries transgressed in your family? Be specific.

3. Who were the people in your family of origin who transgressed your boundaries?

4. Who "pushes your buttons" today in your adult life? What does that feel like?

5. Read the following scriptures and write what they illustrate about the healthy boundaries God demonstrates for us. Can you find others?

   Isaiah 55:8

   Deuteronomy 5:29

   Ezekiel 16:58

   Proverbs 3:12

   Job 5:17

   Hebrews 5:7-9

   Hebrews 12:7-11

EBENEZER II
HOME STUDY
CLASS 2

1. Where have I been carrying "loads" for others that were not mine to bear?

2. What is my motivation to do that?

3. Who do I find it hard to say "no" to? What do I think will happen if I do say "no"?

4. Whose boundaries am I not respecting? How am I transgressing their boundaries?

5. What can I do to change that behavior? Remember that this behavior is rooted in wrong thinking and believing lies. What lies am I believing?

6. If my boundaries are a solid wall, what do I need to build a gate into my wall?

7. If my boundaries are non-existent, what do I need to do to put up a fence with a gate?

EBENEZER II
CLASS 3 AND 4
INTIMACY, TRUST AND CONTROL
CLASS OUTLINE WITH TEACHER'S NOTES

Intimacy, trust and control are all BOUNDARY issues.

Q. Can we have an intimate relationship with someone if we are not a defined person with a sense of "being" who we really are?

If there is no "you", how can there be a "we"?

I. What IS intimacy? How would you define emotional intimacy?

Intimacy means we can be who we are in a relationship and allow others to do the same, without needing to control, fix or change the other person. Intimacy is a delicate balance between separateness and connectedness. We can have intimate relationships if we can:

1. Present a balanced picture of both our strengths and our vulnerabilities

2. Make clear statements of our beliefs, values and priorities, and then keep our behavior consistent with these.

3. Stay emotionally connected to significant others even when things get intense.

4. Address difficult and painful issues and take a position on matters that are important to us.

5. State our differences and allow others to do the same.

This is a tall order! How are you doing?

These five things are a picture of respect for the other person as an individual and for yourself.

Why is each of these difficult for us?

How is this different from the way our childhood families related to one another?

Why is this so much more difficult to pull off than it sounds!?

As children, we had roles to perpetuate the family's dysfunctions, addictions. No one was allowed to be oneself. The family system was rigid and controlled. The system was not dynamic; there was no change, no choices and a loss of self-hood.

Look at each of the 5 behaviors necessary for intimacy separately and discuss why each would be impossible in a severely dysfunctional home.

THAT WAS THEN. WHAT ABOUT NOW?

We've already seen how we have carried our coping mechanisms from surviving childhood right into our adult lives; hence the trunks we continue to drag around with us, our baggage that drags down our lives now.

Under any kind of stress or anxiety, we revert to our relational "coping" mechanisms: pursuing, over-functioning, under-functioning, other-focus, perfectionism, distancing, numbing. When we are still "under the influence" of our dysfunctional families, we usually have **TWO WAYS** of relating to others:

1. **REACTIVITY:** We focus on the other person/people's needs, problems to the exclusion of our own *in order to avoid our own.*

2. **DISTANCING:** We avoid, stay superficial, hide from others. This is actually just another form of reactivity; without boundaries and a sense of self, we are *always reacting to others. We're not in the equation! This is withdrawal.*

What does a grounded, healthy, whole and intimate relationship look like? And how do ours measure up?

Read Romans 12:9-21 and Romans 12:3-5.
Sincere, truthful, honoring, serving God, seeing ourselves with God's eyes

Q. What do you think of the comment, "It seems easier to BE GOD than to LOVE God; easier to CONTROL people than to LOVE people."

Loving them is letting them be who they are. How easy or difficult is that to do?

II. CONTROL FREAKS

What do control freaks have to do with intimacy? Why are we talking about this?

Because control freaks *are death to intimacy in relationships*.

What do control freaks look like?

Well, we could probably get t-shirts made that say "CONTROL FREAKS R US" and be telling no lies!

1. Often first born, is exaggerated if one has younger same-sex siblings.
2. One or both parents often are emotionally or physically unable to do his/her job of parenting.
3. Control freaks know what's best not only for themselves, but for everyone else as well.
4. Move in quickly to advise, fix, rescue and take over when stress hits.
5. Have difficulty staying out of other person's problems and allowing others to struggle with their own problems.
6. Avoid concern or worry about own personal goals and problems by focusing on others.
7. Have difficulty sharing their own vulnerable, under-functioning side, especially with those people they deem have problems. They always present a "strong" facade. They believe the lie that a functioning, whole person does not HAVE an under-functioning, needy side.
8. A control freak may be labeled as "always reliable", "always together", "perfect".

WHY do we tend to over-function and control?

1. Feelings of extreme vulnerability. Everyone feels vulnerable in this world, but those of us who grew up in traumatic, unsafe environments can really feel the need to fix and control those around us and our environment. We are looking for a sense of safety.

2. Fragile self-confidence. Without a sense of personhood and boundaries, we're lost floating in the confusing sea of life. If we can make life feel more predictable by trying to control people around us and the environment, then we feel safer. If we are looking for others to define us (co-dependent stance) then we must control how they see us.

3. Fear. Outside of our relationship to God, fear is the natural response to this world. We tried to control our fear about what was happening to us as children by our behavior and skewed beliefs; as adults we seek to quell the fear in the same way.

Read Proverbs 29:25: "Fear of man will prove to be a snare, but whoever trusts in the Lord will be kept safe."

Charles Spurgeon said, "Anxiety does not empty tomorrow of its sorrow but only empties today of its strength."

Billy Graham said, "Anxiety is the natural result when our hopes are centered on anything short of God."

WHY is it so hard to stop over-functioning and controlling?
Over-functioning and controlling are exhausting, drive other people away and are death to intimacy so why is it so hard to stop?

1. We grew up thinking it was expected of us. This was how our family functioned; we knew fear, not boundaries. Parents and other siblings required parenting by us.

2. We grew up where we didn't feel safe.

3. This was modeled for us in our family; we come from a long line of control freaks! Think about your own family of origin: who is in your line-up?

4. Controlling is a way of managing our anxiety. It is a way of "self-medicating". Move the furniture, alphabetize the spice rack, scream at the kids.

5. Controlling is a way of avoiding our own issues....such as anxiety! If we focus on everyone else and their shortcomings we can avoid seeing-or feeling!- our own.

6. We are used to controlling and change is SCARY. As one woman put it,

"I didn't want to move out of hell. I knew the name of all the streets."

Change is scary, but consider Hebrews 11:8. By faith, (trust in his God-His care) Abraham "obeyed and went, even though he did not know where he was going."

CONTROLLERS ARE PEOPLE WHO DO NOT RESPECT OTHER PERSON'S BOUNDARIES.

Instead of taking responsibility for their own life, they focus on others and seek to control others. How does that square with Matt. 7:3-5? –"Why do you look at the speck of sawdust..."

You might be sitting here not relating to this whole control thing, but hang on! You just might begin to see it differently.

CONTROLLERS CAN BE BROKEN DOWN INTO THREE GROUPS:

1. **"AGGRESSIVE CONTROLLERS'"**: This group is not aware that other people have boundaries. Read Mark 8:32-33-Peter transgresses Jesus' boundaries and Jesus doesn't

allow Peter's rebuke to stand. Instead he exerts his boundaries and rebukes Satan-"Out of my sight, Satan!" People who are chronic advise givers and "fixers" are aggressive controllers. "The surest way to be deceived is to consider oneself cleverer than others."

2. **"MANIPULATIVE CONTROLLERS[2]"**: This group tries to *persuade* people out of their boundaries. They talk others into "yes". They indirectly manipulate circumstances to get their way. "Oh well, if you can't do it then I'll just get someone else who really cares." Jacob in Genesis 25:29-34 is an example of using cleverness to avoid another's boundaries.

3. **"COMPLIANT CONTROLLERS[3]"**: They cannot say "no". They seek to have their own needs met by doing a "favor" for someone in order to be loved. This can look like love and ministry but the truth can be *fear and manipulative motivation*. God looks on the heart.

III. OVER-FUNCTIONING - FACETS OF CONTROL AND PERFECTIONISM

What is over-functioning?
- Over-functioning is when a person is always strong, always able, always in control.
- Over-functioning is when a person always steps in and takes over, "producing" for everyone else.

- Over-functioning is when a person seeks to control his/her surroundings and other surroundings and people
- Over-functioning is death to intimacy!

WHY is it so difficult and painful to stop over-functioning?

1. The over-functioner is unaware of the problem. Always <u>saw</u> it, always <u>did</u> it, this is the norm. It looks better on ourselves than it does on other people!

2. We don't know how to be any different. See #1.

3. It is emotionally painful to change because depression, anxiety, anger rush to the surface. The urge to fix things, or distance when we can't fix things is a form of running from reality and our feelings.

4. It is scary to share our own vulnerability and to relate to another's competence. We are uncomfortable seeing and feeling our own buried unmet dependency needs and longings; needs that used to be blocked by chronically over-functioning and over-focusing on the problems of others.

5. We still believe the lie that having needs is wrong. We still believe the lie that we are required to be perfect in order to be accepted. Hence we need to always come across as functioning perfectly-for ourselves and for others.

And to top it all off, others begin to expect us to over-function for them and this serves to feed our habit pattern and guilt feelings when we try to stop. No wonder this is hard!

ANXIETY PLAYS A BIG ROLE IN CONTROL AND OVER-FUNCTIONING ISSUES

Read I Peter 5:6-11 and I Peter 3:8-9.
How is this NOT the portrait of the controlling, over-functioning fixer?

NEW T-SHIRT FOR THE OVER-FUNCTIONER:

"DON'T JUST DO SOMETHING - STAND THERE!!!!!!!!!!"

IV. WHY IS TRUST A BOUNDARY ISSUE?

Evaluate this statement: "We equate trust with being vulnerable because we lack healthy boundaries."

Without boundaries and a sense of self, trust becomes all or nothing, black and white. Without boundaries we are left totally open, trusting without discernment, trusting people who cannot deliver.

Who *should* we trust?
Psalm 118:8-9

Romans 15:13

Isaiah 2:22

Psalm 112:7

Proverbs 13:20

Psalm 145

We can fully trust in God Himself alone. As we take small steps testing another person's trust-worthiness, our trust is ultimately in God. You might picture looking through the other person to God who is ALWAYS faithful and working for our good.

How are trust and control related?

Having grown up in an unsafe environment, we cope with feeling unable to trust by control-ling and being controlled. We are drawn to relationships where either we can control or be controlled in order to feel safe.

[TEACHER'S NOTE: Invite the class to share how they relate this concept to their own lives.]

How can we change this pattern?

1. Be aware of the issues.

2. Pray without ceasing. Phil. 4:6-"Do not be anxious about anything, but in every-thing, by prayer and petition, with thanksgiving, present your requests to God."

3. Read the Bible. The truth is in the Word. Proverbs. 3:5-6- "Trust in the Lord with all your heart and lean not on your own understanding; in all your ways acknowledge Him and He will make your paths straight." Boundaries are about truth.

4. Surround yourself with "safe" people you can practice boundary issues with as in a support group. Changes come with truth and the Spirit helping us practice the truth. We need one another to practice on! Ecclesiastes 4:9-10-"Two are better than one because they have a good return for their work; If one falls down, his friend can help him up."

EBENEZER II
HOME STUDY
CLASS 3

1. What is my biggest struggle in trying to have intimate relationships with others?

2. What did I learn in my family of origin that sabotages my attempts at intimacy in my adult life?

3. Where and with whom in my life am I caught up in the habit of over-functioning and controlling?

4. How do these people react/feel about my controlling ways?

5. How does it feel to think about letting go of that control? Why would I want to do that? (let go)

6. What does intimacy have to do with healthy boundaries?

EBENEZER II
HOME STUDY
CLASS 4

1. What kind of a controller am I? Am I aggressive, manipulative, or compliant?

2. What examples can I think of that illustrate that?

3. What things inside me seem to drive me to over-function for others?

4. God is the only person completely trustworthy. Meditate on the following passages:

   Psalm 118:8-9
   Psalm 112:7
   Psalm 145 (all)
   Isaiah 2:22
   Proverbs 13:20
   Romans 15:13

5. How are my problems with trusting others and controlling others related? How does this problem manifest itself in my life?

EBENEZER II
CLASS 5 AND 6
CRISIS ORIENTED LIVING AND OBSESSIVE-COMPULSIVE BEHAVIOR
CLASS OUTINE WITH TEACHER'S NOTES

"I USED TO KNOW EXACTLY WHAT I WANTED AND WHERE I WAS GOING WITH MY LIFE, BUT IT WAS ALL A COVER, A LIE. I WAS USING MY DRIVES, ABILITIES AND RELATIONSHIPS TO HIDE FROM THE HURT. NOW I'M CONFUSED. I SEE THAT ALL OF THAT IS SUPERFICIAL BUT I FEEL EMPTY. IF I'M NOT THE PERSON I USED TO BE, WHO AM I?[1]"

We can get through these 14 Ebenezer classes and start to feel just this way-
"Out with the old but *WHAT* IS THE NEW??"

Talk about the quote. Does anyone identify with the person who wrote it?

What does this person mean?

How do you think Jesus would answer this question?

Maybe He would say, "Come to me all you who are weary and burdened and I will give you rest. Take My yoke upon you and learn from me for I am gentle and humble in heart. You will find rest for your souls, for my yoke is easy and my burden is light." Matt.11:28-30

When we get to this stage of recovery, we need to ask ourselves:
Do we want to live in the truth or hide in the lies?

God is about making something new. Read II Corinthians. 5:17

"Therefore if anyone is in Christ, he is a new creation; the old has gone, the new has come."

It is important to settle, at this point, who it is that we are following because we are about to really open up and allow God to meddle in our lives.

When we begin to seriously look at the coping mechanisms that we have clung onto all our lives as if our very lives depended on them, it takes tremendous courage to forge ahead. These coping mechanisms can be like tent pegs; if we stop using them, the old tent collapses. God wants to build a new tent.

Those "coping mechanisms" can be behaviors we practice regularly.

When we come from severely dysfunctional homes, we tend to create crisis and get "stuck" in behaviors that we continue to repeat and that actually make life more difficult.

Why do we do this?

1. It is habitual-these are old coping mechanisms we used to survive. They are habits.

2. We are more comfortable with the familiar. Crisis feels familiar; change is scary.

3. It is a diversion tactic; we can avoid the truth, change and reality by creating crisis and habitually practicing obsessive-compulsive behaviors. We "make friends" with the escape. It feels good, we may not have immediate unacceptable consequences.

4. Our old coping mechanisms that make up our obsessive-compulsive behaviors don't "work" now-they create crisis and more problems. So we practice more obsessive-compulsive behaviors in order to avoid truth and pain and thereby create more problems....and the cycle keeps repeating.

The cycle looks like this:

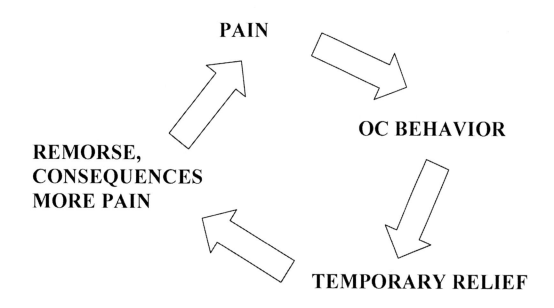

PAIN

OC BEHAVIOR

**REMORSE,
CONSEQUENCES
MORE PAIN**

TEMPORARY RELIEF

Obsessive-compulsive behaviors are a trap. Which of these has been a trap for you?

Control

Facades: hide self, avoid relationships, avoid conflict

Alcohol, substance abuse, prescription drugs

Food-under-eating, overeating

Anger: avoid intimacy, create crisis

Sex: numbing, feelings of power, control

Shopping, overspending: diversion, feelings of power

Worry-especially about everyone else!

Approval seeking: numb our self-doubts

Success, power: facades, numb self-doubts, feelings of power

Pleasure as escapism: numbing, escape, diversion

Exercise: feelings of power, control, numbing, seeking a "high"

Workaholism: success, control, approval seeking, power

Computer games: numbing, diversion

Recovery work: surprise! Escape from the "real world" and mature responsibility

Religion: power, control, black and white thinking, security

Hypochondria: avoid emotional and behavioral issues by focusing solely on physical

You fill in the blank!

ANYTHING USED IN EXCESS AND IN THE WRONG WAY IN ORDER TO NUMB OUR PAIN can become an obsessive-compulsive behavior for us.

This is why I said that it takes tremendous courage at this point in our recovery journey.

It is essential that we make God our refuge and not look to escapes in order to ease our pain.

When we turn to these escape behaviors instead of God, we make them an idol.

Webster's defines idol as: "An object of extreme devotion".

Read I John 5:20-21-we need to be in Him who is true.

Read Psalm 73:21-28. If our eyes stray from God and his Truth, we are like the Psalmist Aseph when he says, "When my heart was grieved and my spirit embittered, I was senseless and ignorant; I was a brute beast before you."

He ends by saying, "I have made the Sovereign Lord my refuge."

It is important to make God our refuge and not look to idols to ease our pain.

We need to make the decision that God will be the strength of our heart and our "portion"; what we have, what we want. Seeing how our childhood affected us is the *beginning* of our recovery; making this decision to seek and cling to God is the *hope and meat* of our recovery.

This is a conscious choice.

Jude 24 and 25: "To **Him who is able to keep you from falling** and to present you before His glorious presence without fault and with great joy-to the only God our Savior be glory, majesty, power and authority, through Jesus Christ our Lord, before all ages, now and forevermore! Amen."

Who, or what, is able to keep us from falling?
Is it anything from the above list of obsessive-compulsive behaviors we use to staunch the pain? Is it the lies we have believed?

In the words of Francis Schaeffer, "How then shall we live?" How shall we go forward to health and wholeness?

[**TEACHER'S NOTE:** Read Ephesians 4:17-5:20. If there is sufficient time, break into small groups to list what can be found in this lengthy passage about how we are to live.
If time does not allow, suggest this exercise be done at home, on our own.]

1. Our thinking has to change-"be renewed"
2. Put off falsehood-look at the truth
3. Put on the new self-created to be like God, in His image, be imitators of God
4. Live in the Light of Truth

This is NOT about willpower but *transformation.*
If we put our trust in our own willpower to overcome and be different, we are doomed to failure. We will keep repeating the same cycles of escape and destruction. Our hope is in our Savior and His Spirit to transform us and free us from the idols of escape.

[**TEACHER'S NOTE:** The following page is the homework to be completed before the next class. Instruct the class to read the example of an obsessive-compulsive behavior, in this case, *exercise*. Ask them to identify an OC behavior of their own and to list things about their behavior that make it an OC behavior.].

EBENEZER II
CLASS 5 AND 6
IDENTIFYING OBSESSIVE-COMPULSIVE BEHAVIORS

Addict Quiz: Using the example of "Exercise"

"Exercise" could be an obsessive-compulsive behavior if:

- You work out or exercises every day even if you are ill or sore
- You often do back-to-back aerobics classes
- You enjoy the muscle pain after pushing yourself to the limit
- The more you work out, the more you find body parts to fix
- If you miss a work-out, you do double the next day
- You have a history of training injuries
- You would rather spend time exercising than with family
- You are losing interest in other activities
- No matter how much weight you lose, you see a fat person in the mirror
- You feel guilty any day you don't work out
- Your whole life and feeling of purpose is centered around your exercise activity
- If you recognize three or more of these symptoms, you may be obsessive-compulsive with exercise

Identify an OC behavior of your own. An OC behavior is something you use to avoid truth, pain, and God. Now, similar to the *exercise* example, (e.g. control, food, alcohol, spending, approval seeking, work, etc.) list things about your behavior that make it an OC behavior.

EBENEZER II
HOME STUDY AND MEDIATATION
CLASS 5

1. Where do I think I am in my "recovery process" from my painful childhood? In other words, have I passed through the identifying stage where I look at my story, am I still in the thick of mourning and grieving, am I working on forgiving and letting go? Or am I still looking at all of this intellectually and holding it away from myself?

2. What progress have I made in "feeling my feelings"?

3. Am I really ready to co-operate with God in changing my heart and my life? What am I still clinging onto?

4. What does my own "Cycle of Pain" look like? What do I do habitually in order to ease my pain? What havoc does this create in my life?
    Create a drawing to illustrate your cycle if you can.

5. Do I want to live in the truth or continue to hide in the lies? Read Jeremiah 10:11-16. Meditate on what it means to put other things before God. How am I doing that in my life?

EBENEZER II
CLASS 7 AND 8
RELATIONSHIPS-EXPLORING HOW OUR SPECIAL DYSFUNCTIONS CHALLENGE OUR MARRIAGE
CLASS OUTLINE WITH TEACHER'S NOTES

When asked, "Why do you want to be close to another human being?" women from severely dysfunctional homes reply:

1.   "So I won't be lonely"

2.   "So I won't feel unlovable."

3.   "So I won't feel afraid."

If she was more aware of her deeper feelings, she might also say,

1.   "So I can continue in the same comfortable, familiar patterns as my childhood family."

2.   "So I can finally be happy."

3.   "So that all my unmet needs will be met."

4.   "So that I can finally be loved, get attention"

5.   "So I can change the other person and finally get it right"

Is there anything wrong with this perspective?

THIS KIND OF THINKING IS LIKE TWO TICKS, EACH LOOKING FOR A HOST!

Do you think marriage will solve these problems?

Where do these needs come from? Will marriage take care of them?

When we grow up in a severely dysfunctional home, we come with a boatload of childhood unmet needs, perhaps the belief that our needs are not allowed, and no concept of how to do something about these needs.

More baggage we may carry into relationships is the expectation that **OUR** marriage and **OUR** family will be better, different from, (perfect!) our family of origin.
Or that our relationships with other people will be naturally and automatically different from our family of origin, and nourishing to us, unlike our childhood home.

These women above are saying, in effect, "I want an intimate relationship to fix my childhood."
It will not take long into the relationship or marriage to see that this is a fantasy. If those are our expectations, then the reality is painfully devastating.
How deep and painful do you think these unmet childhood needs really are?

The problem with looking to the relationship to fulfill all those needs is that the focus is on oneself, and probably the other person is coming with their own trunk load of unmet needs for YOU to fulfill!

Discuss how each of the listed traits (remember from Ebenezer I?) of a survivor of a severely dysfunctional home affects our relationships, marriage, and the quest for intimacy:

1.   Fear of losing control-so we become controlling
2.   Fear of feelings, unawareness of feelings (numbness)-how can we be emotionally present for others if we are numb?
3.   Fear of conflict (unable to have or express needs, non-revealing fake façade)-how can we be intimate if we do not present our genuine self?

4. Over-developed sense of responsibility/Over-functioning (controlling, resentful, transgressing boundaries, unable to relax and have fun)

5. Feelings of guilt when standing up for self instead of always giving in to others (no defined sense of self)-living life as a "blob"

6. Inability to relax and have fun (drill sergeant)- part of our control issues

7. Harsh self-criticism (defensive, self-focused)-depressed, weary

8. Living in a world of denial (presenting a false self)-unable to work through normal conflicts in the relationship

9. Difficulties with sexuality (unresolved issues from childhood sexual abuse, confusion)-fear, flashbacks or promiscuity

10. Living life from the standpoint of a victim (self-focus, looking for trouble)-a chip on the shoulder

11. Compulsive behaviors (escaping issues, feelings, consequences)-self and other destructive behaviors creating crisis diversions

12. Reacting instead of acting (focus on other person to exclusion of self and own contribution)-fear of presenting genuine self, hyper-sensitivity

13. More comfortable with chaos instead of security and peace (creating problems to escape real issues or intimacy)-fear of getting close and being rejected, unloved

14. Fear of abandonment (clinging, smothering, pushing away)-if I don't get close, they can't leave me

15. Black and white perspective under pressure (no room for compromise, flexibility)-need for control and sense of safety

16. Physical complaints/stress related illness-somatization, impaired immune system

17. Backlog of delayed grief (with underlying depression, suppressed rage, withdrawal, numbness, lack of joy)

18. Underlying old rage (anger sticking out all over the place-tone of voice, expression and body language, outbursts)

19. The ability to survive (loyalty, never giving up, inner strength)

20. In recovery, the unique ability to appreciate being loved and loving at the deepest level-because it was lacking in our childhood, if we experience being loved in adulthood, it is a treasure

Old messages play in our heads everyday. After discussing the following three, name others and how they intrude on your marriage. These are messages that were given to us by our caregivers as we grew up, messages we give to others in our relationships, and perhaps messages now given to us by the significant people in our lives.

1.   I love you/ Go away

There is no consistency in an unhealthy home. Parents are absorbed with worry, personal problems, and addictions. Ever wonder why you are attracted to that person who is warm and loving one day and rejecting the next?

The pattern feels familiar. There may be an unconscious desire/plan to fix the other person's problem and "get it right' this time by repeating the pattern.

Because we come to our relationships with abandonment issues, we can alternate between smothering, clinging and blaming, and withdrawal and erecting walls.

We long for intimacy and attention with our unmet childhood needs and we cling and smother. We fear these needs won't be met because of the depth of our unmet childhood needs so we withdraw and erect walls or create crisis.

2.   You can't do anything right/ I need you.

As a child, you may have labored under perfectionistic standards. You were never good enough. You believed if somehow you were good enough, things would have been better in your home. Yet often your parents seemed needy and out of control. The roles might have been reversed. As an adult, you may be drawn to relationships that are both dependent and highly critical. Again, that feels familiar. Or you may only SEE them that way because of your background. You may find yourself striving for their approval. When you are treated poorly, you may analyze the situation and "prevent yourself" from feeling angry feelings (numb, stuff, deny) because you don't consider anger to be an allowable feeling. Stuffing the anger causes depression, illness, explosions. You become the perfect doormat for an inconsiderate person.

3.   I'll be there for you/next time

You may have learned not to want or to feel needs so that you can avoid disappointment when the needs go unmet. This is a lose-lose situation in your present life and marriage which generates a fear of self-disclosure (intimacy) and asking for what you want. If you ask and don't get, this proves too familiar and uncomfortable. The result is that you may require your friend/spouse to be a mind-reader who will automatically know what you need and want. That spells disaster in light of how differently men and women think!

Expressing needs is the highest and most important gateway to intimacy.

4.   Everything is fine/How can I deal with all this?

Growing up, there was an underlying sense that all was not OK and that something was expected of us to make it right. We adopted the thinking that we CAN and we WILL take charge. Our motto might be, "If it MUST be done, then it CAN be done!" (not true) Or simply, "It's all up to me."

We were required to take on roles and responsibilities that were beyond the abilities of a child. We were required to understand and process, without help, situations that were too much for our developmental stage.

We may still function as adults believing these lies, over-functioning for others, often with underlying resentment.

Talk about how it makes you feel to begin to see the similarities between your choice of friends or mate and your childhood family system.

The question is:
How can we begin to change the old messages in our head?
How can we begin to change the way we relate to our friends/husband that is driven by our particular traits that are a part of our old coping mechanisms?

[**TEACHER'S NOTE:** Divide class into 5 groups, each taking one of the following points, discussing it and presenting findings to the group.]

1. We see them (the coping mechanisms) for what they are and begin to see where they come from. We begin to identify the lies we have been believing and replace them with the truth. Give some personal examples.

2. We do the steps of recovery from Ebenezer I
    *   Talk
    *   Grieve
    *   Replace lies with God's Truth
    *   Adopt a new identity in Christ
    *   how are these steps helping or not helping your process of change/recovery?

3. Remember it is WORK and a process, not an instant fix. Are we committed to Christ for the long haul? Romans 8:28-39

    What gets us bogged down? Make it personal.

4. Remember who is in charge and who owns our life. Jeremiah 10:23 and 24

    What happens when we forget? Make it personal.

5. Replace old messages with new.

    A. Get to know the Word. Romans 12:2

    B. Enlist help of your friends/spouse. Work together to change. Work with a counselor skilled in family systems.

    C. Know what love is. Study God's definition and seek the help of the Spirit to learn how to love. Romans 12:9-21

What experience have you had in doing these three steps? What was difficult? Where were your victories? What plans can you make to work through these?

EBENEZER II
HOME STUDY
CLASS 7

1. What am I looking for in my most emotionally intimate relationship?

2. Which ones of my personal traits from surviving a traumatic childhood have most affected my relationship? How have each impacted the relationship?

3. What old messages from my childhood have played in my head as an adult? How might I still be hearing these messages from my current relationship?

4. Think about these messages. How much of what we think we are hearing is really being said or implied and how much of it is our old filter miss-reading the messages?

Talk about this with your friend/spouse.

EBENEZER II
HOME STUDY
CLASS 8

1.   How do I feel about taking ownership of the way my own issues from my childhood have impacted my marriage? (Or close relationships)

2.   Where do I think I am in the recovery process now? As I consider the steps of Talk, Grieve, Replace lies with God's Truth, and Adopting a New Identity in Christ, do I think I am making progress? Where am I "stuck"?

3.   Think of specific examples of moments in your relationship that illustrated how your recovery work has made a difference and how you made a different choice when relating because you have been doing the work of recovery. How did your spouse react?

4.   Which of the old messages from childhood have impacted you and your marriage most? What is the lie in this message and what is the truth that you want to begin substituting into the old message?

EBENEZER II
CLASS 9 AND 10
INTIMACY AND CONFLICT RESOLUTION
CLASS NOTES WITH TEACHER'S NOTES

How did we define intimacy?

We can be who we really are in a relationship and then allow others to do the same, without needing to control, fix or change the other person. Intimacy is a delicate balance between separateness and connectedness.

The following are levels of intimacy Gary Smalley describes in his book, *SECRETS TO LASTING LOVE*[1]? (see page 29)
Describe each and give examples from your own experience in friendship and marriage if you can.

1. Speaking in clichés-"Hey, how are you? Fine."

2. Sharing facts-"The garbage needs to go out."

These two are the "dance of conflict". The relationship stays at this level because this is the safe zone. About many marriages you could say, "They don't have twenty years of marriage, they have one year twenty times."

3. Sharing opinions   The door to intimacy-here the risk begins!

4. Sharing feelings   The stakes just went up!

5.   Sharing needs   The ultimate vulnerability

Why is sharing opinions the conflict barrier?

Because as we share opinions, it becomes *personal.* There is now room for:

1.   "Critical remarks[2]" (That's not right!" "You always do it wrong!")

2.   Condescending remarks[3]" ("You are so stupid!", "Do you see what an irrational statement that is!") Labeling the other person.

3.   The return to safer levels[4]" (How was your day? Fine.)

Talk about how these are related:

    1.   Acceptance
    2.   Our definition of intimacy (see above)
    3.   The conflict barrier (sharing opinions)
    4.   Honoring

It's a no-brainer that there WILL be conflict in every marriage. Where there are two different people, there will be two different ways of being and thinking.

Our definition of intimacy requires us to accept and honor the other person in the relationship. As we honor and accept one another, there is now room for different opinions. "Different" is a friendly conflict so we can pass through the conflict barrier of sharing opinions unscathed. "Different" is vastly *different* from WRONG!

Conflict= "Mental struggle resulting from opposing needs, drives, wishes." Webster

Discuss this statement, as quoted by Gary Smalley[5] of Dr. Gary Olive, in light of the above:

"Conflict is the price we pay for intimacy"

If we are going to be in an intimate relationship where opinions and needs are routinely expressed, the two inevitably different people must know how to negotiate the shoals of conflict. Without acceptance and honor, the boat will hit the reef and sink.

HONOR

What do you think of the statement, "You can learn all the marriage skills you want, but without reverence, awe, respect and admiration (honor) it doesn't work."[6]

That's because our underlying attitude is going to come out. The words we say, our tone of voice, the rolling of our eyes or the exasperated sigh that escapes our lips.

How would you define "honor"?

Webster says, "Respect and esteem shown to another."

Smalley says, "Profound respect mingled with love, devotion and awe."

"Honor is the act of recognizing, respecting, and loving *your mate's DIFFERENCES*[7]"

How much easier it is to respect and esteem your friend's/mate's similarities!

Discuss the statement, "Honor isn't merely important to the relationship; it's absolutely critical. Without honor, you cannot attain intimacy in a relationship; moreover it is impossible to create even a functional relationship without honor. Honor has to be the center…"[8]

How do we show honor? Gary Smalley suggests:

1. **Make a decision** to value and accept the differences of the other person, leading to an attitude of submission. Learning to *treasure* our friend's differences!

2. **Listening without defenses** and the need to "fix"-this attitude comes from *embracing* the differences.

3. **Communication-without anger**, asking for help in understanding. A non-defensive stance without a shield of self-protection. Listening in love. REALLY listening.

4. **Combining differences / opinions** instead of eliminating one. Not so much COMPROMISE as COLLABORATE. There is peace when one compromises with the other; there is STRENGTH when the two are both contributing. Forget compromise!

5. **Nurturing** by offering:
   a) deep seated security
   b) meaningful conversation
   c) emotional or romantic times
   d) positive physical touching

READ THE FOLLOWING SCRIPTURES AND RELATE THEM TO OUR DISCUSSION:

1. **Ephesians 4:29-32**

No unwholesome talk, only that which is helpful for building up.

No bitterness, rage anger…

Be kind and compassionate, forgiving

Honoring, communication, nurturing, listening

2.   Ephesians 5:21

Submit to one another

Honoring, collaborating

3.   Philippians 2:1-4

Doing nothing out of selfish ambition

In humility consider others more important

Honoring

4.   I Corinthians. 13:4-13

Definition of love

Honoring, communication, listening, non-defensive

Recognizing dishonor

Gary Smalley says, "Dishonor can be subtle, but I have learned to look for a mental 'red alarm'. Anytime you feel that you are superior to your mate, that your thinking is more valid, your concerns are more important, your talents are better, your expectations are more accurate, you instantly send yourself straight back to the cold side of the wall of conflict and to more superficial levels of intimacy.[9]"

How to disagree with honor

We said forget compromise and go for collaboration. How do we disagree and both contribute?

1. **"Control your anger[10]."** GS says this is the biggie; the nuclear bomb of relationships. See again how important it is to be "current" with our feelings; dealing with the sealed in rage from childhood in recovery and learning to experience our feelings day to day as they occur. Here's the formula: Honor first, then act/speak. If we could get a hold on that one, just think how differently these arguments would go!

    A wise friend I know, Dr. Mark Good, says the best sentence to keep at the tip of our lips when we disagree is, "You may be right about that."

2. **"Constantly remember, and reinforce, your honor[11]."** Instead of blaming and venting, learn to consciously and continually give your friend/mate priority over these strong emotions of anger and frustration.

    Think of the person first, before the issue. The relationship is more important than the issue.

3. **"Ask for help[12]."** Instead of reacting, ask questions and seek to understand your friend's/mate's heart. Ask for clarifications to help you see from their perspective.

A great line is, "So, I think what you are saying is…."

4.   **"Look for the win-win solution[13]."** Both your feelings, opinions are valid. Look to collaborate, not eliminate. Look for solutions where neither of you sacrifices your opinions, feelings and needs.

       Think of yourselves as a team, both on the same side.

[**TEACHER'S NOTE:** Read the following article together as a class and discuss.]

HONOR AND DISHONOR ARTICLE

Where do you see honor/dishonor in this article by Benna Sherman, psychologist.

"The day before had started off so nicely. Melanie and Mark had spent the day wandering around the botanical gardens. It was pretty, it smelled good, and he's held her hand much of the time. They'd laughed together, made fun of the sillier looking people, and had a delightful time together.

It was part of their plan to return the warmth and romance to their marriage. They'd hit a rough patch and were now committed to getting over it with greater emotional intimacy than they'd had before.

After hours of warm closeness, they'd returned home and re-entered their more familiar roles and routines. Unfortunately, they'd also repeated an old and troublesome pattern.

As Mark entered the house, he'd dropped Melanie's hand, walked over to the television and turned it on. She felt dropped, ignored and rejected. After a day of such delightful close-ness, it was particularly painful to feel like she'd been replaced by a grown-up version of a crib mobile.

What's more, she reverted to an old pattern of hers. Instead of saying something to Mark at the time, she'd bit her lip, swallowed her disappointment and gone off to find something to do by herself.

However, she'd gotten up this morning with a new resolve to approach her hurt feelings differently. Years of swallowing her hurt and anger had left her bitter toward and estranged from Mark. As part of her commitment to nurturing their new closeness, she'd been determined to share with Mark what she was feeling so that they could work through the event together.

She'd waited for a reasonable time to talk to him, invited him to a private conversation out of earshot of the kids, and said there was something she needed to share with him.

She'd told him that out of respect and trust for his statements of commitment to her, she wanted to share with him how upset she'd been the evening before upon their return home. She's told him what she had felt and how very sad and discouraged it had made her.

Mark immediately went on the defensive. He moved rapidly from explaining his behavior to defending his character. He insisted that she had no right to feel what she was feeling, that he was innocent of any malicious intent, and that frankly he was angry himself at being accused so unfairly. He loudly and forcefully pointed out several things that she'd done that he felt justified his behavior.

It was at this point that Melanie mumbled, "Fine", and left the room.

Mark was the one left standing in command of the room and, he felt, the conversation. As the adrenaline receded, however, he felt less and less like a victor. He really was committed to Melanie and to this marriage, and he knew that his defensive posture had just done significant damage to both. Gathering his courage and commitment, he walked into the kitchen to find Melanie nursing a cup of tea at the table.

'Mel, could we try that conversation again? I'm pretty sure that I can do a better job.'
'What's the point, Mark? You either don't understand or don't care.'

'Mel, I am sincerely requesting that you help me to understand. I will listen to everything you have to say; and I don't want you to stop talking until you're convinced that I have heard and understood everything you want me to.'

'But you'll just defend yourself and maybe even attack me, like you always do.'
'Mel, I just defended myself up, down and sideways. I'm acutely aware that I have not won an argument but lost a bit of my wife. I swear, I can learn to do this differently. Please give me a chance.'

Melanie started, very tentatively, to try to explain how she felt about the TV thing. She kept watching him to see if he was really listening, really not becoming defensive. He listened intently, interrupting only to ask clarifying questions, and expressed his understanding of her feelings. She kept waiting for him to stop her so that he could explain why she was wrong. It never happened.

At the end, when she affirmed that she felt he understood, she asked him why he'd changed gears after all this time of doing it the defensive way.

'Well, Mel, I love you. I want to be with you. I don't want to make you sad or hurt. Defending myself wasn't getting me any closer to my goals and it was sending me further from you. It just seemed stupid. I think it's probably a natural reaction, but I think I finally figured out that it's not a useful one between two people who love each other.'"

The Evening Capital
Benna Sherman

EBENEZER II
HOME STUDY
CLASS 9

1.   When I think about the levels of intimacy as described by G. Smalley, what level do I
      think my marriage (friendship) usually achieves?

2.   How do I feel about differences and conflict in my marriage (relationships)? Do I see
      them as positive or a threat?

3.   How successful are we in sharing opinions, feelings and needs with one another? What
      do I do to sabotage that level of intimacy?

4.   What practical changes can I make in the way I relate to my spouse (friend) so that I
      might better show honor to him or her?

EBENEZER II
HOME STUDY
CLASS 10

1.   What do my disagreements look like with my spouse (friend)? Think of a recent example. In what ways did I show dishonor toward him/her?

2.   What is REALLY most important to me: the issue we are disagreeing about or the person with whom I am in conflict?

3.   Think through what you would like to share with your spouse (friend) about what you are learning about emotional intimacy and conflict. Concentrate on your own part in this; ways *you* would like to change, how you see that *you* have contributed to being stuck in non-intimate ways of relating to one another. Keep the focus completely on yourself. Then make a date to talk together about what you are learning. Ask your spouse/friend to pray for you as you submit yourself to the Spirit making changes in your thinking and behavior.

THE EBENEZER
PROGRAM

EBENEZER III

EBENEZER III
WOMEN SUPPORTING WOMEN
STATEMENT OF PURPOSE

Ebenezer III is a ministry for women who have graduated from the Ebenezer I and II programs and who are seeking to grow in their relationship with Christ by practicing the Biblical truths studied in class. Ebenezer III is an environment where women can practice taking risks of self-disclosure and love with other women who understand the struggle. Meetings are held monthly. Participants volunteer to act as "presenters", whose responsibility is to choose a topic for presentation/study/ and discussion at group. The comfort level of the individual determines the extent of preparation and presentation made by the "presenter". The "presenter" may simply choose the topic, allowing the group to do the preparation and discussion or the "presenter" may study and prepare thoughts for the group. We can ask the tough questions because we seek answers from the Lord God and His wisdom.

While confidentiality is an important tenet of the group, it must be understood that there is no guarantee that a group member will not break this understanding. This is a *safer environment, not a perfect one.*

ESSENTIAL TO OUR GROUP IS:

1.   OPENNESS IN SAFETY

Galatians 5:13-"You, my brothers, were called to be free. But do not use your freedom to indulge the sinful nature; rather serve one another in love."

James 3:3-5- "When we put bits into the mouths of horses to make them obey us, we can turn the whole animal. Or take ships as an example. Although they are so large and are driven by strong winds, they are steered by a very small rudder wherever the pilot wants to go. Likewise the tongue is a very small part of the body, but it makes great boasts. Consider what a great forest is set on fire by a small spark."

Free to speak, remembering that Christ is present.

Free to speak, remembering to keep confidentiality.

2.   FELLOWSHIP OF COMFORT

II Corinthians. 1:3-7- "Praise be to the God and Father of our Lord Jesus Christ, the Father of compassion and the God of all comfort, who comforts us in all our troubles, so that we can comfort those in trouble with the comfort we ourselves have received from God. For just as the sufferings of Christ flow over into ours lives, so also through Christ our comfort overflows. If we are distressed, it is for your comfort and salvation; if we are comforted, it is for your comfort, which produces in you patient endurance of the same sufferings we suffer. And our hope for you is firm, because we know that just as you share in our sufferings, so also you share in our comfort."

Free to comfort as we are comforted.

3. DESIRE TO GROW AND HONOR GOD

Philippians 3:10-14- "I want to know Christ and the power of His resurrection and the fellow-ship of sharing in His sufferings, becoming like Him in His death, and so, somehow, to attain the resurrection from the dead."

Free to forget what is behind and press on toward what is ahead.

4. SEEK TRUTH

John 3:21- "But whoever lives by the truth comes into the light, so that it may be seen plainly that what he has done has been through God."

John 8:32- "Then you will know the truth, and the truth shall set you free."

God is the truth that sets us free.

5. PRACTICE THE TRUTH

Hebrews 5:11-14- "We have much to say about this but it is hard to explain because you are slow to learn. In fact, though by this time you should be teachers, you need someone to teach you the elementary truths of God's word all over again. You need milk, not solid food! Anyone who lives on milk, being still an infant, is not acquainted with the teaching about righteousness. But solid food is for the mature, who by constant use have trained themselves to distinguish between good and evil."

James 1:22-25- "Do not merely listen to the word, and so deceive yourselves. Do what it says. Anyone who listens to the word but does not do what it says is like a man who looks at his face in the mirror, and after looking at himself, goes away and immediately forgets what he looks like. But the man who looks intently into the perfect law that gives freedom, and continues to do this, not forgetting what he has heard, but doing it-he will be blessed in what he does."

Free to grow toward maturity.

EBENEZER III
FACILITATOR'S GUIDE

Ebenezer III is designed to be a safe place to practice the truths learned in Ebenezer I and II. The structure is much looser and is directed by a facilitator instead of a teacher. The graduates from previous years are invited to choose topics of interest to them and then how those topics are explored is entirely up to them. Some ambitious persons will make more of a presentation while others may choose to simple throw out the question or topic to be discussed. The responsibility of the facilitator is to keep the discussion on track by encouraging everyone to participate and endeavor to focus the group on God's truths.

It is helpful to have every member of the group sign up for a week and a topic in advance. This seems to result in all members feeling part of the group and also serves to give participants advance notice of the topics to be explored so as to provide time to give thought to the discussions to come.

My thinking is that Ebenezer III provides a bridge from the somewhat self-focused stage of recovery to operating in the world at large. It is a place where we can practice relating to others without wearing the façade of perfection. We can practice maintaining healthy boundaries, saying "no" and refraining from transgressing the boundaries of others by "fixing" them.

Sometimes the transition from the group that has weathered the storms of Ebenezer I and II together to the larger Ebenezer III proves rocky. The class may feel afraid to let in "outsiders" who are strangers to them. This, however, can be an opportunity to take the next step from ingrown recovery work to growing up and serving God in the world around us. The facilitator can encourage the group to see this challenge and move forward.

The following are two topics as examples. The first is more of a presentation and the second an example of a question format.

EBENEZER III
TOPIC I
WHERE WAS GOD THEN????

Suffering through childhood abuse, when we were helpless and unable to protect ourselves, can leave us with questions about the existence of evil and the goodness of God. The questions plague us: "Where was He then? Didn't He see? Didn't He care?"

We are left trying to trust a God who "let us down". No one may have shown themselves trust worthy in our young lives so how are we to learn so foreign a concept? In order to survive, we practiced the habit of control. If no one else was coming to our aid, then we would nail it all down ourselves.

We live in a world with a very skewed concept of life. Without conscious thought, we have bought into the whole distorted picture.

So, what is the truth? And where do we find it?

There are three main areas of lies that cause us to come to conclusions that separate us from God and lead us into sinful attitudes and behaviors. These are:

- View of self
- View of God
- View of the world.

Only by taking in the whole of God's truth in His word will we be able to change our distorted beliefs.

VIEW OF SELF

We can go through life believing a pack of lies about ourselves.

- I'm a target. "They" are out to get me, to hurt me.
- Nobody understands me. I am alone and abandoned.
- My problems are someone else's fault. I blame them.
- I have to be right. There is no room for being wrong.
- I have to punish them, make them pay.
- I deserve for things to go well. I have a right to happiness.
- I deserve to have it MY way.
- Life should be fair. Especially MY life!

All these lies are based on the BIG LIE that the world is all about *us*. The world is here for me, God is here for me and I know the way things should be.

We don't want to suffer and we want anyone who causes us to suffer to pay.

"One woman told me, "All my life, I've felt that somebody-God, my family, or someone-owes me something to make up for all the hurt I've experienced. Whenever things went well, I felt vindicated. Not happy, really, but vindicated. Happiness and vindication are different; one is relaxed and content; the other is proud and defiant I lived with the constant fear that I wouldn't get what I deserved. I tested people to see if they were 'for me or against me.' When something didn't go well, or when people didn't give me the attention I 'deserved' (or demanded!), I felt like the old wound was torn open again. So many situations and people seemed unfair because I demanded so much from them. I expected them to balance the scales of justice and to give me the love and contentment I really wanted. Demanding what I 'deserved' seemed right and fair, but it was unrealistic. It led to more bitterness and resentment if my needs weren't met, and pride and greater demands if they were." Getting Unstuck, by Robert S. McGee and Pat Springle

Part of feeling that we deserve fairness, happiness and ease is the natural, sinful reaction to suffering at the hands of another. We want revenge, retaliation, and the scales to be balanced. "If God wasn't there THEN and He didn't stop the abuse, the least He can do now is help me balance the scales with them." Except the scales are *ours*, not God's.

In Isaiah 40:25-28 it says:
"To whom will you compare me? Or who is my equal?" says the Holy One." Lift your eyes and look to the heavens: Who created all these? He who brings out the starry host one by one, and calls them each by name. Because of His great power and mighty strength, not one of them is missing. Why do you say, O Jacob, and complain O Israel, "My way is hidden from the Lord; **my cause is disregarded by my God"?** Do you not know? Have you not heard? The Lord is the everlasting God, the Creator of the ends of the earth. He will not grow tired or weary, and His understanding no one can fathom."

"The penchant for justice is a two-edged sword. Though we demand it for those who have hurt us, we won't admit that if WE received justice, we would be in trouble! Our focus is on those who have wronged us instead of our sins toward others. We must realize that we are not only victims, but victimizers as well." Getting Unstuck

We want it *our* way. God's plan is frequently not our plan. And *our* plan **never** includes suffering!

VIEW OF GOD

We often transfer problems with earthly authorities (particularly parents) onto our relationship with God.

Parents who were harsh and abusive can lead us to view God as demanding and cruel, untrustworthy.

Parents who were aloof and neglectful may cause us to see God as uncaring and absent.

We may articulate all the right theology of God's love and character, but our most deeply held convictions may be just the opposite.

- God isn't "fair"
- If God is all-powerful, He could have stopped the abuse, the pain
- He won't come through for me now when I need Him
- I have to do everything just right in order for Him to help me
- He is using the abuse to punish me
- I know what I need and if He doesn't provide what I need, then He isn't trustworthy
- When I suffer, God is not with me

When we suffer, we ask, "Where is God? Why doesn't (didn't) He rescue me?" When I suffered my physical and emotional breakdown in 1987, I had the same reaction. We start out looking like we are trusting God, but the longer and deeper the suffering goes, the greater the struggle to trust in God's goodness.

I started out with what I *thought was trust,* but the more pain I felt, the more silence from God I heard, the quicker my cries came, "Where ARE you? Have mercy! Make me well! Take this away!"

After a time I heard a quiet "Trust me." I learned that my version of trust was founded on *circumstances* and my understanding of them, rather than on the character of God.

Much of what can LOOK like trust in an afflicted person is really just the confident expectation of restored blessing. "It's OK-God will take this away and everything will be fine again."

I started with "I trust you God. Make me well."

I moved on to "Have mercy. Make me well! I want the old me back. I want my life back."

When God had done His work, my words changed to "I am yours. Make me whole-whatever that means."

There was a subtle but-oh-so important shift in my attitude, my perspective about what was going on and who was in charge.

If we are to understand suffering and just where is God when we're doing it, we need to understand the **character of God and the presence of God.** Janet Erskine Stewart said, "Joy is not the absence of suffering, but the presence of God."

When the Psalmist said "I will fear no evil.." was it because

- There is no evil
- Evil couldn't touch him?

No, we live in an evil, twisted world where there is suffering and death.

The Psalmist says "For Thou art with me" I will fear no evil because God's presence is with me. When we suffer profoundly and come to the end of ourselves, everything else is wiped away except the presence of God.

Why this? Why me? Why now? Why then?

When we focus on trying to understand the mind of God instead of on His character, we become confused. As God said to Job, "Who is this that darkens my counsel with words without knowledge? Where were you when I laid the earth's foundation? …Have you ever given orders to the morning, or shown the dawn its place?. Have the gates of death been shown to you? What is the way to the abode of light?. Surely you know, for you were already born! You have lived so many years!…."

When Job sees his own arrogance in trying to "out-think" God, he says, " I know that you can do all things; no plan of yours can be thwarted. You asked, 'Who is this that obscures my counsel without knowledge?' Surely I spoke of things I did not understand, things too wonderful for me to know….My ears had heard of you but now my eyes have seen you. Therefore I despise myself and repent in dust and ashes."

The only appropriate response to the character of God is worship. Trying, insisting, on understanding the mind of God and demanding our way is sin; Larry Crabb calls this attitude "demandingness".

VIEW OF WORLD

- Life should be fair
- People should be kind and good
- My life should be happy and easy

How many of us, without giving it any examination, believe these three declarations? On what do we base our view of the world?

Is life fair? Read Matthew 5:44-48 and Acts 7:54-8:3

Are people kind and good? Romans 7:14-20, Ecclesiastes 9:3, Romans 3:10-18

Is life happy and easy, all the time for everyone? John 16:33, Ephesians 6:12

What does Malachi 3:13-4:3 say about the ultimate justice and fairness of our God?

In all recorded history, mankind has been asking God the same question: "Where were you THEN? Where are you NOW?" Read Judges 6:12-16.

The right view of the world and our place in it is found in Psalm 73.

QUESTIONS FOR THOUGHT

(Taken from *Getting Unstuck* by Robert S. McGee and Pat Springle)

1. How were you actually a victim? In what ways do you continue to feel/act like a victim?

2. How do people take revenge on others to try to punish people, aggressively or passive-aggressively? Which do you use?

3. What lies about yourself, God and the world have taken hold deep within you?

4.   In what ways have hating and blaming others, those who hurt and abused you, and God, given you a sense of power?

5.   What truths about yourself, God and the world will you take hold of now?

6.   What passages of Scripture have been most helpful to you on this topic?

EBENEZER III
TOPIC II
TRUST AND CONTROL

1.   Discuss: "If you cannot trust, you have to control"

2.   Read Isaiah 14:27 and 8:13-17. What do these passages say about our ability to control God?

3.   Is God "safe"?

4.   Discuss the difference between safe vs. good and controllable vs. trustworthy.

5.   How would you define blind trust, lack of trust and perceptive trust?

6.   What is at the core of a control freak?

7.   Discuss: "The soul of control is fueled by anxiety and nurtured by feelings of extreme vulnerability and a fragile self-confidence"

8.   Discuss: "Anxiety is the natural result when our hopes are centered on anything short of God." Billy Graham

9. Discuss: "Some people spend their entire lives indefinitely preparing to live."

10. After looking at the heart issues, here are some practical ways to practice taming the control freak inside us:

   - Slow down-recognize hurry sickness
   - Reduce your anxiety level. Look hard at how much you are running as escape. Is fear, strong feelings, anger causing you to drive yourself for escape and escalating stress? Where can you practice letting go of something/one? When can you practice being still and knowing He is God?
   - George Miller said, "The beginning of anxiety is the end of faith; and the beginning of faith is the end of anxiety."
   - Grit your teeth and delegate. Sure it won't be as good as we would do, but that's our control freak talking!
   - Give up the "if onlys". Stop looking back with regret that "it" wasn't perfect. Nothing is and neither are you.
   - Defer to others whenever you can. Ask others ideas and opinions and then really listen. It's the uncontrolling thing to do.
   - Do one thing at a time. Give up multitasking.
   - Admit when you are wrong.

11. Discuss how perfectionism and trust and control relate to one another?

   ➢ **The following pages contain quotations, writings and poems that can be used for discussion or personal encouragement and growth.**

"In this world you will have troubles. But take heart, I have overcome the world!"

Jesus Christ
John 16:33

ANYTHING BUT THAT

"Send anything but that", I cried,
And still the thing I feared did come;
I watched its shadow rise
And shrank in terror from the blow:
"Oh, Lord, this thing I cannot bear!"

And yet Thy tender love did send it me
In answer to my prayer.

My prayer! My cry Thou heedest not
And leav'st me sick, in pain.
And still Thy presence sears and binds-
Is all my praying vain?
And still it comes, this fearful dark;
I cannot stem the tide.
"No more", I cry, "I know my strength!"
And then, Thou, God replied,
"Thy frenzied strength thou knowest, ah
But thou dost not know Mine."

Barbara Black
1987

"Is the pain in my own life all waste? Has no strength or even sweetness sprung out of my past sorrow? And when I look back on my sins, may I not sing Te Deum Laudamus (We praise Thee, O God) for all the pride they overthrew, all the humility they fostered and all the gentleness and sympathy they begot. God has led me through many ways not of my choosing-now high, now low-now in broad daylight, now in midnight gloom, and now in pelting storm. Yet though I am evil, He is good; and great, yea, omnipotent in goodness, since He has drawn good from the heart of evil, and He will build a home of everlasting life on the ruins of sin."

Bede Garret, O.P.

"All my gashes cry: Alleluia!"

C.S. Lewis

THE THORN

"There was given to me a thorn in the flesh"
II Corinthians 12:7

When gifts and graces Thou didst give
With breath of life to all who live,
Wherewith to work for Thee,
A strange and bitter dower was mine,
For in Thy providence divine
A thorn Thou gavest me.

While others serve Thee, glad and strong,
And life aloft faith's triumph-song,
And scale the heights for Thee,
I walk alone a hidden way,
My sole companion night and day,
The thorn Thou gavest me.

Oh, days are lonely, nights are long,
And far the light, and faint the song-
And yet I worship Thee;
And faithfulness and grace I ask
To work with patience at my task-
The thorn Thou gavest me.

And when I see Thee as Thou art,
One humble gift my burning heart

Would bring in love to Thee:

Bedewed by tears, enriched by blood,

I'll hand Thee back, in fragrant bud,

The thorn Thou gavest me.

Margaret Clarkson from Grace Grows Best in Winter

THE TERROR OF THE NIGHT

In the darkness demons hover
Shredding at my sanity.
Memories are present nightmare
Laughing, jeering, "Where was He"?
Disobedience alluring
Poisoned trap of death and lies,
Every breath a bloodstained passage
Thought a nest of restless knives:
Dreaming dies.

Lord, I doubt Thy sweet provision
Lord, I blame Thee for the years
Empty, searching, wasting, wanting-
Lord, I blame Thee for my tears.
Now the fear I really fear is
Hardened heart immune to grace
Fighting wisdom, choosing space:
My own place.

You are testing, sifting, probing,
Saying that I have the strength.
Still my soul weeps yearning, wretched,
"Lord, I have no strength for Thee!"
Nothing left to trust or wonder,
Holding fast to misery,
Longing for one moment's honest

"Abba, succor, rescue me!"

Only Thee.

Am I so gone I cannot turn again

And know a lover's joy?

Though lost in fear of Thee, the God I've wronged,

I cannot doubt Thy heart.

But come, ashamed and broken, caked with ash

To plead for Thy regard

And find Thy hand has held me all along.

Barbara Black

1990

CONSOLATION

"When sorrow comes under the power of Divine grace, it works out a manifold ministry in our lives. Sorrow reveals unknown depths in the soul, and unknown capabilities of experience and service. Sorrow is God's plowshare that turns up and subsoils the depths of the soul, that it may yield richer harvests…Hence it is sorrow that makes us think deeply, long and soberly. Sorrow makes us go slower and more considerately and introspect our motives and dispositions. It is sorrow that opens up within us the capabilities of the heavenly life; that makes us willing to launch our capabilities on a boundless sea of service for God and our fellows. God never uses anybody to a large degree until after He breaks that one all to pieces."

Letty Cowman

FOOTNOTES

Ebenezer I

Class Outline with Teacher's Notes

Class 1 and 2

1. Sandra D. Wilson, *Released From Shame*, Intervarsity Press, Downers Grove, Illinois 60515, 1990. p.43.
2. Ibid.p.43.
3. Ibid.pp.37-38.
4. Daryl E. Quick, *Healing Journey For Children of Alcoholics*, Intervarsity Press, Downers Grove, Illinois, 60515, 1990.p.34-35.
5. Sandra D. Wilson, *Released From Shame*, Intervarsity Press, Downers Grove, Illinois 60515, 1990.pp.46-48.
6. Ibid.pp.53-53.
7. Ibid.p.82.
8. Ibid.p.83.
9. Ibid.p.83.
10. Ibid.p.84.

Ebenezer I

Class Outline with Teacher's Notes

Class 3

1. Sandra D. Wilson, *Released From Shame*, Intervarsity Press, Downers Grove, Illinois 60515, 1990.pp.26-29.

2.   Ibid.p.28.

3.   Ibid.pp.26-29

4.   Ibid.pp.26-28

5.   Ibid.pp.39-40

6.   Ibid.p.65.

7.   Ibid.p.65.

8.   Ibid.p.66.

9.   Ibid.p.66.

10.   Ibid.p.68.

11.   Ibid.p.68.

12.   Ibid.p.29.

13.   Ibid.p.29.

14.   Ibid.p.29.

15.   Ibid.p.29.

Ebenezer I

Class Outline with Teacher's Notes

Class 4

1.   Sandra D. Wilson, *Released From Shame*, Intervarsity Press, Downers Grove, Illinois 60515, 1990.p.95.

2.   Ibid.p.95.

3.   Ibid.p.97.

4.   Ibid.p.99.

5.   Ibid.p.99.

6.   Ibid.p.99.

7.   Ibid.p.99.

8.   Ibid.p.96.

Ebenezer I

Class Outline with Teacher's Notes

Class 5 and 6

1. David E. Frye, *Griefwork and the Adult Children of Alcoholic Families*, Thomas W. Perrin, Inc., Rutherford, New Jersey 07070, 1986. p.1.

2. Ibid.p.1.

3. Daryl E. Quick, *The Healing Journey For Adult Children of Alcoholics*, InterVarsity Press, Downers Grove, Illinois 60515, 1990. p.79.

4. David E. Frye. *Griefwork and the Adult Children of Alcoholic Families*, Thomas W. Perrin, Inc., Rutherford, New Jersey 07070, 1986. p.8.

5. Ibid.p.8.

6. Robert S. McGee and Pat Springle, *Getting Unstuck*, Rapha Publishing/Word, Inc., Houston and Dallas, TX. 1992. pp.111-112.

7. Ibid.pp.113-114.

8. Ibid.p.168.

Ebenezer I

Class Outline with Teacher's Notes

Class 7 and 8

1. Robert S. McGee and Pat Springle, *Getting Unstuck*, Rapha Publishing/Word Inc., Houston and Dallas Texas, 1992.p.168.

2. Ibid.p.166.

3. Ibid.p.166

Ebenezer II

Class Outline with Teacher's Notes

Class 1 and 2

1. Dr. Henry Cloud and Dr. John Townsend, *Boundaries,* Zondervan, Grand Rapids, Michigan 49530, 1992.p.29.
2. Ibid.p.31.
3. Ibid.p.31.
4. Ibid.pp.31-32.
5. Ibid.p.32.
6. Ibid.p.33.
7. Ibid.p.30.
8. Ibid.p.31.
9. Ibid.p.42.
10. Ibid.p.43.

Ebenezer II

Class Outline with Teacher's Notes

Class 3 and 4

1. Dr. Henry Cloud and Dr. John Townsend, *Boundaries,* Zondervan, Grand Rapids, Michigan 49530, 1992.p.54
2. Ibid.pp.55-56.
3. Ibid.pp.59-60.

Ebenezer II

Class Outline with Teacher's Notes

Class 5 and 6

1. Robert S. McGee and Pat Springle, *Getting Unstuck*, Rapha Publishing/Word, Inc., Houston and Dallas Texas, 1992.p.91.

Ebenezer II

Class Outline with Teacher's Notes

Class 9 and 10

1. Gary Smalley, *Secrets To Lasting Love, Uncovering The Keys To Life-Long Intimacy*, Simon and Schuster, New York, New York, 10020, 2000.p.29.
2. Ibid.p.47.
3. Ibid.p.48.
4. Ibid.p.48.
5. Ibid.p.97.
6. Ibid.p.128.
7. Ibid.p.134.
8. Ibid.p.128.
9. Ibid.p.155.
10. Ibid.p.161.
11. Ibid.p.161.
12. Ibid.p.161.
13. Ibid.p.162.

CPSIA information can be obtained at www.ICGtesting.com
Printed in the USA
237868LV00002B/10/P